PAINTING CANADA

TOM THOMSON AND THE GROUP OF SEVEN

PAINTING

CANADA

TOM THOMSON AND THE GROUP OF SEVEN

PWP

First published in 2011 by
Philip Wilson Publishers
an imprint of I.B.Tauris & Co Ltd
6 Salem Road
London W2 4BU
www.philip-wilson.co.uk

ISBN Hardback: 978-0-85667-708-3
ISBN Softcover: 978-0-85667-686-4

Distributed in the United States and Canada
exclusively by Palgrave Macmillan
175 Fifth Avenue, New York NY 10010

Edited by Amy Concannon
For PWP: David Hawkins

Design by Anne Sørensen and Design Execution
Printed in Italy by Printer Trento

This book has been produced to accompany
Painting Canada: Tom Thomson and the Group of Seven,
an exhibition organised by Dulwich Picture Gallery
and the National Gallery of Canada, in collaboration
with the National Museum of Art, Architecture and Design,
Oslo and the Groninger Museum.

With the generous support of the McMichael Canadian
Art Collection and the Art Gallery of Ontario.

Presenting Sponsors

 RBC Wealth Management

Media Partners

Supported by

 KINNEAR
FINANCIAL LIMITED

We would also like to thank the Timothy Franey
Foundation, The Funding Network and Farrow & Ball.

pp. 60–61:
Tom Thomson
Maple Woods,
Bare Trunks (detail)
Winter 1915–16
Oil on canvas
81 x 87 cm
Private collection

Contents

Acknowledgements

Curator
Ian A.C. Dejardin

Co-curators
Katerina Atanassova
Anna Hudson

*Exhibition management
at Dulwich Picture Gallery*
Sarah Clarke
Amy Concannon

*Exhibition tour management
at the National Gallery
of Canada*
Karen Colby-Stothart
Christine Sadler
Christine LaSalle
Alana Topham
Diane Watier

*Director of Development
and Communications at
Dulwich Picture Gallery*
Lily Harriss

*Chair of the Trustees of
Dulwich Picture Gallery*
James Lupton

*The exhibition has been
supported by:*
The Board of the Canadian
Friends of Dulwich Picture
Gallery
David P. Silcox (Chair)
Ian A.C. Dejardin (Director)
Lily Harriss (Secretary)
Paula Dimond (Treasurer)
Phillip Crawley
Martha Durdin
Rupert Duchesne
Gregory Kane, Q.C.
Michael Koerner
A.K. Prakash
Ashley Prime
F. Mark M. Fell
With thanks also to
Robert Reymond, Richard Self
and Donna Thomson

*Canadian Friends of
Dulwich Picture Gallery:*

Major Supporters
Dasha Shenkman
A.K. Prakash
Nancy and Richard Self
Renae and Michael Tims
Lois and Rod Green
Sarah and Mark Evans
George C. Estey

Director's Circle
Sonja and Michael Koerner
Adrian Burns and
Gregory Kane, Q.C.
Beverly and Fred Schaeffer
Holly Coll-Black and
Rupert Duchesne
Sotheby's Canada Inc.
Masters Gallery Ltd.

Curator's Circle
Alison Fisher
Martha Durdin
and J. Anthony Caldwell
Dawn and Mark Fell
Joan F. Ivory

*We would like to thank the
following for their contributions
to the exhibition:*
Alison Beckett, Julian Beecroft,
Sbrenka Bogovic, Stephen Borys,
Anna Brennan, Janine Butler,
Janet B. Cauffiel, Emma Conner,
Heather Darling-Pigat,
Gary Essar, George C. Estey,
Barbara Fischer, Michael Foster,
Norm Francis, Charles C. Hill,
Ruth Gaskill, Emily Goalen,
Rod Green, Grace Hailstone,
Rob Haine, Gary Haines,
Jerome Hasler, Sally Hayles,
Greta Hildebrand, Gregory
Humeniuk, Scott James, Mariëtta
Jansen, Paula King, Ross King,
Karen Kisiow, Steve McNeil,
Masters Gallery Ltd., Annick
Lapôtre, Linda Louwagie-
Neyens, Ellie Manwell, Catharine
Mastin, Brian Meehan, Linda
Morita, Nils Ohlsen, Benjamin
O'Connor, Leanne Pepper,
Julie Pickard, A.K. Prakash,
Lisa Quirion, Liana Radvak,
Christopher Régimbal,
Jane Rhodes, Dennis Reid,
Denise Ryner, Beverly and
Fred Schaeffer, Stew Sheppard,
Rosemary Shipton, David P.
Silcox, Michael Stevenson,
Maria Sullivan, David Thomson,
Lizzie Watson, Sean Weaver, the
Wyndham Lewis Memorial Trust
and the private collectors who
wish to remain anonymous.

We are also grateful to the
Canada House Arts Trust and
the Canadian Friends of Dulwich
Picture Gallery for their
enlightened support of a year-
long Canadian Artist in Residence
at Dulwich Picture Gallery.

Forewords

Given the Group of Seven's desire to break the bonds that tied the art of Canada to that of Europe and England, it is ironic that this nationalist art movement would achieve recognition at the British Empire Exhibition at Wembley in 1924. Following years of bitter public debates at home about the value of Canadian modern art, the movement was now approved for Canadians by the British press. Yet the artists were always more conscious than their Canadian audience of their position within broader international art currents. It was an exhibition of Scandinavian art shown in Buffalo in 1913 that provided inspiration to J.E.H. MacDonald and Lawren Harris, and foreign recognition was one of the goals in their efforts to affirm that Canadians had something unique to contribute to the larger world of art.

If the paintings by Group members stole the limelight in 1924, there have been surprisingly few opportunities for English audiences to see large collections of their paintings since, save for two exhibitions organized by Michael Tooby, then Director of Sheffield's Mappin Art Gallery, in 1991. Now thanks to another British admirer of the Group, Ian Dejardin, it is with great pleasure that the National Gallery joins with Dulwich Picture Gallery to present this outstanding exhibition marking the bi-centenary of Dulwich's establishment and to share these paintings with the Groninger Museum in Holland (a first) and the The National Museum of Art, Architecture and Design in Oslo.

Our sincere thanks to the dynamic team at Dulwich Picture Gallery. It was a pleasure to collaborate with them on this exhibition, and more specifically, with Ian Dejardin, Director, Sarah Clarke, Head of Exhibitions, and Amy Concannon, Exhibitions Officer.

Thanks also to the venues and their staff, under the direction of Patty Wageman, Director International Exhibitions, Groninger Museum, Groningen, and Nils Ohlsen, Director of Old Masters and Modern Art, The National Museum of Art, Architecture and Design, Oslo.

At the National Gallery of Canada, this project was led by the solid expertise of Karen Colby-Stothart, Deputy-Director, Exhibitions and Installations, with the assistance of Charles Hill, Curator, Canadian Art, Stephen Gritt, Director, Conservation and Technical Research, John McElhone, Chief, Conservation, Susan Walker, Paintings Conservator, Jean-François Castonguay, Chief, Technical Services, Christine Sadler, Chief, Exhibitions Management, Christine La Salle, Exhibition Manager, Diane Watier, Art Transit Coordinator, and Alana Topham, Loans Coordinator.

All of us are delighted to see these exceptional examples of Canadian art reach an ever-broadening audience.

Marc Mayer
Director and CEO, National Gallery of Canada

Way back in the late 1980s, when I was a curatorial assistant at London's Royal Academy, I stumbled on a book in the library there, about the Group of Seven. I had never heard of them before and fell in love on the spot. Over twenty years later, I am delighted, and not a little amazed, that Dulwich Picture Gallery should be the first to mount a show dedicated to Tom Thomson and the Group of Seven.

To this day, the influence of Thomson and the Group of Seven on Canadian art is profound – even if that influence is rejected, most Canadian artists have to at least grapple with this particular sacred cow at some point before proceeding. For most of the twentieth century, and continuing into the twenty-first, the Group of Seven have been discussed, dissected, dismissed, and rediscovered by Canadian scholars and public, to the point of exhaustion. Yet their visual legacy remains supremely powerful: many Canadians, raised with reproductions of the Group of Seven's most famous paintings on their classroom walls, still see their own country through the Group's eyes.

That is what makes the prospect of an exhibition in Europe so exciting. In England, and on continental Europe, none of this baggage pertains. Relatively few people in England have heard of Tom Thomson, or of Lawren Harris, J.E.H. MacDonald, A.Y. Jackson, Arthur Lismer, Frank Johnston, Franklin Carmichael and Frederick Horsman Varley (and those that have tend to be practising artists); our response to their paintings is unadulterated by the decades of debate, free of the burden of over-familiarity or too much knowledge. We can respond directly to these paintings as paintings – their colour, their dynamism, their power, their painterliness, and their sheer beauty. Then again – unlike in Canada – the landscapes these artists chose to paint are also unfamiliar. Few of us in Europe could point more than vaguely on a map to any one of the locations these artists depicted. These are painted woods, trees, lakes and mountains only. Nonetheless, non-Canadians should be aware: we are on holy ground.

Ian A.C. Dejardin
The Sackler Director, Dulwich Picture Gallery

Painting Canada
Tom Thomson and the Group of Seven

Ian A.C. Dejardin

Setting the Thames on fire[1]

In 1924 and 1925 at the British Empire Exhibition in Wembley, London, displays of Canadian art received an enthusiastic reception. Of the 270 works shown in 1924, covering the whole spectrum of Canadian artistic output from academic to cutting edge, it was the more modern artists that attracted most attention. Of particular note were a small group of canvases by Tom Thomson (1877–1917) and the artists who had, in 1920, begun to exhibit collectively as the Group of Seven: Lawren Harris (1885–1970), J.E.H. MacDonald (1873–1932), A.Y. Jackson (1882–1974), Franklin Carmichael (1890–1945), Frederick Horsman Varley (1881–1969), Frank Johnston (1888–1949) and Arthur Lismer (1885–1969) (fig. 2, overleaf). The critics characterised the artists' achievements as new and exhilarating while not so extreme as to be off-putting. As the Saturday Review said: 'The Canadian artists are more independent of prevailing fashions than the younger English, while they are as remote from the academic'.[2] Another wrote: 'Nothing could be less academic… and at the same time less freakish'.[3] The British critics would perhaps have been surprised to discover how these same artists had been reviewed by critics in their native Canada. In a canny marketing move for their next exhibition in Toronto, opening 8 January 1925, the Group took out an advert contrasting the British reaction with what they were used to from their home team of critics:[4]

'They are garish, affected, freakish'
Toronto Star

'A single narrow and rigid formula of ugliness'
Saturday Night, Toronto

'A school of landscape painters who are strongly racy of the soil'
London Times

'The foundation of what may become one of the greatest schools of landscape painting'
Morning Post, London

The Canadian critical response in general had not in fact been entirely negative – there was some positive appreciation among the brickbats – but the Group seem to have dwelt on their martyrdom at the hands of their local press. This was their fauve moment (the term, meaning 'wild beast', famously applied to Matisse, Derain and others at the Salon d'Automne in 1905) and artists intent on change may prefer to be seen as outrageous revolutionaries (until starvation or privation looms, at least); but the more measured British response did better capture what was remarkable about the work.

The Group of Seven may have been modernists in the sense of deliberately setting out to reject outmoded academic ideas and replace them with something new, but storming barricades for the sake of it was not what they were about. Their style could be described as late post-impressionist with symbolist and expressionist overtones; elements of arts and crafts sensibilities are seen from time to time,

Fig. 1
Tom Thomson
The Jack Pine (detail)
1916
Oil on canvas
127.9 x 139.8 cm
National Gallery of Canada,
Ottawa, purchase 1918 (1519)

Fig. 3
Augustus John
The Blue Pool
1911
Oil on panel
Aberdeen Art Gallery
and Museums

Fig. 4
Derwent Lees
The Blue Pool
1911
Manchester
City Galleries

and, as the 1920s advance, there is the occasional hint of art deco – enough to remind us that most of these artists were also professional graphic designers. Compared with what was happening in contemporary France, however, the Group of Seven look conservative. The more extreme Canadian critics' responses – one was famously reminded of the contents of a drunkard's stomach when contemplating a MacDonald painting,[5] while another invented the term the 'Hot Mush School'[6] in reference to work by Jackson – seem ludicrous now and were reactionary even then.

So successful was the 1924 British Empire Exhibition for the Canadians that they were invited back the next year. The 1925 selection featured twenty-four pictures by Thomson and the Group, including MacDonald's *October Shower Gleam* (cat. 78), Thomson's *Spring Ice* (cat. 8) and *The Pointers* (cat. 13), and Johnston's *Algoma Arabesque* (cat. 65), the latter three returning for display in London now for the first time since then.[7] There was a second showing from 26 November to 23 December 1925, at the Whitechapel Gallery in London's east end. The foreword, culled from the Wembley catalogue, pinpointed the works' 'qualities of originality, frankness, and an indigenous Canadianism'.[8]

Parallels for the work of Thomson and the Group of Seven were to be found in England and elsewhere. At around the same time the Canadian artists were starting to produce their first notable works, one of England's most famous artists, Augustus John, was painting landscapes, often in Wales alongside Derwent Lees and James Dickson Innes (figs. 3 and 4), which have much in common with their Canadian counterparts. They have a similar intensity of colour, reliance on quick, *en plein air* sketching and sense of immediacy. These British artists were also searching for a visual language to conjure up a particular landscape; as John put it, he was looking for 'the reflection of some miraculous promised land',[9] in his case of sunny childhood memories of Wales. Meanwhile, in London, the Camden Town Group had formed in 1911, and although their principal interest was painting urban scenes, they also produced landscapes – and in the bright, high-toned work of Robert Bevan, Harold Gilman and Spencer Gore a further echo of the

Fig. 5
**Sir John Arnesby
Brown, R.A.**
The Raincloud
c. 1915
Oil on canvas
63.5 x 76.5 cm
Royal Academy of
Arts, London

Fig. 6
Ferdinand Hodler
**Lake Thun and
the Stockhorn
Mountains**
1910
Oil on canvas
83 x 105.4 cm
Scottish National
Gallery of Modern Art

Canadian modernists can be found. Even a more
traditional Royal Academician such as Sir John
Arnesby Brown, whose paintings mix an easy
Impressionism with Barbizon styling, could on
occasion produce not dissimilar work (fig. 5).
The latter circumstance is perhaps not as coincidental
as it may seem, given that Arnesby Brown was the
brother of Eric Brown, the then Director of the
National Gallery of Canada, the man who acquired
Thomson's *Spring Ice* (cat. 8) for the Gallery in 1916.

Elsewhere in this catalogue Nils Ohlsen
discusses Scandinavian art, in particular the impact
of the exhibition held in Buffalo in 1913, which
undoubtedly influenced, at least temporarily,
future Group members Harris and MacDonald
(and through them Thomson and Carmichael),
who made the journey to see it. In Scandinavian art
Harris and MacDonald recognised kindred spirits
at work. The paintings by Swiss artist Ferdinand
Hodler (fig. 6) resonate with work done by another
Group member, Frederick Horsman Varley (cat. 101),
and with MacDonald's Rocky Mountain pieces
(cats. 88–97). It is therefore perhaps helpful to view
the Canadian modernist painters in the context of
a global reaction against academism, in which the
examples of impressionism, post-impressionism,
symbolism and expressionism worked as catalysts,
liberating an entire generation of artists to
experiment with colour and technique, revelling
in their new freedom. The Group of Seven can
certainly also be seen as part of a more universal
'northern' cultural phenomenon.

Canadianism

Yet, British critics also recognised something
which set the Canadian painters apart: the
intensity of their identification with their subject,
Canada itself – their 'Canadianism', as the 1925
catalogue put it. The second largest country in
the world geographically, Canada had a tiny
population at that time of just over seven million,
barely the size of one major European city. In the
early years of the twentieth century, the vast
empty spaces of Canada represented adventure
and opportunity to a generation of young men
and women struggling to keep their heads above
water in Europe. Many emigrated, including

Fred Varley and Arthur Lismer (both Sheffield-born), while MacDonald (born in Durham, although his father was Canadian) had moved to Canada with his family at the age of fourteen.

The artistic mission of the Group was always tied to a drive to 'discover' and interpret their vast, little-known and – they felt – under-appreciated homeland. This is what gave these painters their fiery sense of purpose, and it showed in their work. Academic orthodoxy decreed that the Canadian wilderness was too wild, bleak, huge and raw to function as a subject fit for a landscape painter. F.B. Housser, the author of the first book about the Group of Seven,[10] tells us that the same orthodoxy maintained that the native pine tree, the Jack Pine (*Pinus banksiana*), was also unpaintable (it is no accident that some of the movement's greatest masterpieces prove this wrong; see cats. 10 and 52).[11] These extraordinary sentiments emerged from a thorough immersion in European practice – Constable, the Barbizon school, the Hague School – and the American Hudson River School. Tom Thomson and the Group of Seven sought a way to see the Canadian landscape without that baggage.

In some ways, the experience of the war artists (a body which was to include Jackson, Lismer and Varley) was analogous – these Canadian landscape paintings are like reports from a benign frontline, from artists embedded in hard-won new territory. The title of Paul Nash's famous war painting, *We Are Making a New World* (fig. 7), could – shorn of its context and its bitter irony – be meaningfully applied to what the Canadians felt they were doing in the wilds of Algonquin Park, and, indeed, that work reminds us of a particular favourite subject of the Group, one which Thomson initiated in works like *Burnt Land* (cat. 2), recording a landscape shaped not in this case by war, but by the logging industry and fire. Thomson was already dead before Nash produced his picture, but it is perfectly possible that the spectre of blighted war-torn landscapes (which Varley and Jackson also painted) affected the way the Group chose to interpret this theme thereafter; Lawren Harris's stylised tree stumps on the north shore of Lake Superior (fig. 8) have a similar elegiac quality.

Fig. 9
Tom Thomson fishing at Tea Lake Dam
c. 1915
Art Gallery of
Ontario, Toronto

Fig. 10
Tom Thomson
c. 1905
McMichael
Canadian Art
Collection Archives

'A new type of artist': Tom Thomson

To the memory of Tom Thomson
artist woodsman and guide
who was drowned in Canoe Lake
July 8th 1917

He lived humbly but passionately
with the wild. It made him brother
to all untamed things of nature,
it drew him apart and revealed itself
wonderfully to him. It sent him out
from the woods only to show
these revelations through his art
and it took him to itself at last.

His fellow artists and other friends
and admirers join gladly in this tribute
to his character and genius

His body is buried at Owen Sound
Ontario near where he was born[12]
August 1877

This inscription, set into a stone cairn overlooking Canoe Lake, the scene of his death, memorialises Tom Thomson as 'artist woodsman and guide' – to the uninitiated, a rather strange way to describe arguably Canada's greatest landscape painter. To a non-Canadian, the question of whether this great manipulator of oil paint on panel and canvas could find his way in the woods, or lead others safely through Algonquin Park, may seem of little relevance. And yet, this triple-headed description was penned not by a woodsman, or guide, but by J.E.H. (Jim) MacDonald, friend, fellow-artist, poet, author, teacher and founder member of the Group of Seven, a man who, according to A.Y. Jackson, 'was a quiet, unadventurous person, who could not swim, or paddle, or swing an axe, or find his way in the bush'.[13] Of course, the cairn was erected overlooking the very stretch of water where the tragedy occurred, a matter of months after Thomson's death when emotions were still raw, so the mythologising tone is perfectly understandable – MacDonald and his friends knew the significance of their loss. Although Thomson had already achieved quasi-heroic status among his fellow

artists, and indeed sold a couple of paintings to public collections, he was still very much one of the 'rising men' of Canadian art and not by any means famous outside that very limited milieu. Locals of the Canoe Lake area probably had very little, if any, idea what Thomson was up to, dabbing away at small boards with paintbrushes. Those who did understand may still have valued his prowess as a fisherman more; not that Tom would have minded. As Fred Housser put it:

This task [of expressing the spirit of the Canadian landscape in paint] demands a new type of artist; one who divests himself of the velvet coat and flowing tie of his caste, puts on the outfit of the bushwhacker and prospector; closes with his environment; paddles, portages and makes camp; sleeps in the out-of-doors under the stars; climbs mountains with his sketch box on his back.[14]

So it is perhaps not so surprising that Thomson's 'man of the woods and lakes' persona took equal billing to his status as artist in MacDonald's tribute; discovering a visual language to do justice to their great country seemingly required artists to rough it heroically in the wild. When in Toronto, however, Thomson could be rather a snappy dresser, spending more than he could afford on stylish clothes. Though we may visualise him as the 'bushwhacker and prospector' (see fig. 9), his various studio portraits tell a different story (fig. 10), as does the fact that he mixed the contents of an expensive tube of cobalt blue into the standard grey marine paint with which he painted his canoe. For a woodsman and guide, that canoe cut a dash.

Still young, dark, handsome, supremely talented, moody, seemingly oblivious to discomfort, with a reputation as a fisherman and canoeist, spending his summers among the lakes and trees of Algonquin National Park, friends with the park rangers, occasionally earning some extra funds through guiding tourists ... *and painting* – Tom was the very incarnation of the new movement, a movement which very clearly, from the language of the memorial cairn, had heroic aspirations right from the start.

Canoe Lake, 8 July 1917

Thomson died suddenly, 'in mysterious circumstances', in July 1917; the manner of his death and subsequent events effected his metamorphosis into absolute legend as a Canadian hero. The myth developed parallel to, and almost independent of, a steady growth in his posthumous reputation as an artist. To a non-Canadian audience, it cannot be stressed enough just how iconic Tom Thomson is in Canada. Not only the country's most famous artist, the creator of *The Jack Pine* (cat. 10) and *The West Wind* (cat. 12), Canada's most instantly recognisable paintings, Thomson's death has provided the country with an enduringly fascinating mystery, complete with contradictory conspiracy theories, for nearly a century.

There is practically no aspect of the tragedy that cannot be questioned, apart from the stark fact of the death itself and where his body was found on Canoe Lake. Thomson may not, in fact, even have died on 8 July – possibly the evening before.[15] He probably didn't die by drowning – he may have been already dead when he hit the water. His death may well not have been accidental – either outright murder, or at the very least manslaughter, have been suggested. The cause of death may have been a blow to the head, possibly sustained during a fight or in a fall against a fender. The suggestion is that Thomson's body was then dumped in the lake, weighted down by means of fishing line wound round his ankle and attached to a heavy weight; then again the fishing line may simply have been tied to his ankle to tow the newly surfaced body ashore.

Other authorities have offered alternative theories: he committed suicide; or was drunk (Thomson certainly seems to have liked a drink) and fell out of his canoe, hitting his head as he fell; or that he stood up to answer a 'call of nature' and overbalanced, banging his head as he fell.

The mystery of the actual cause of death paled, however, beside what happened afterwards. His body surfaced nine days later, not surprisingly in a terrible state. A rushed post-mortem examination on a nearby island by a local doctor preceded an equally rushed burial in the local Canoe Lake cemetery. A coroner arrived too late to examine the body, but the local doctor had cited accidental drowning as cause of death, and the coroner accepted that (despite some discrepancies, notably a four-inch bruise on Thomson's temple). Then came the news that his family wished him to be buried in the family plot at Leith up by Georgian Bay. So another undertaker was engaged to accomplish the gruesome business of disinterring the body, transferring it to a sealed casket and transporting it to the family. This was done – at dead of night, with no witnesses – and a steel casket was duly delivered to Leith, where it was interred. That is where his gravestone stands, but some believed – and there is evidence to suggest that they were right – that Thomson's body was in fact never moved, and still rests at Canoe Lake.[16]

Seen in the context of an exhibition of his work, none of this really matters except as an explanation of the fascination Thomson holds for a Canadian audience. For the rest of us, the simple fact remains that Thomson was vibrantly alive one minute, producing brilliant work with every promise of more to come, and gone the next, much too young and effectively at the very beginning of his career. He has featured in songs, documentaries, novels, children's stories, ghost stories (inevitably, a mysterious canoeist glides – allegedly – across Canoe Lake), feature films, and countless non-fiction books. He appears in contemporary paintings such as Peter Doig's *White Canoe*, fig. 12 (based on fig. 11, which shows Thomson sketching from his canoe). The founding of two summer camps for girls and boys on Canoe Lake soon after he died has ensured that the legends continue to thrive in impressionable young minds.

Thomson is regularly assumed to have been a member of the Group of Seven, and would certainly have been so, but he died too soon. His friends did his memory justice, however, and his remarkable, brief firework display of talent influenced them profoundly. His work continued to be exhibited alongside theirs: at Wembley and the Whitechapel Gallery in 1925, at the height of the Group of Seven's activity, Thomson was represented by five pieces, more than any of the Group.

Fig. 11
**Tom Thomson
Sketching in a
Canoe**
1914
Photograph
Arthur Lismer papers,
Edward P. Taylor
Research Library
and Archives
Art Gallery of
Ontario, Toronto,
gift of Marjorie Lismer
Bridges (file 19)

Fig. 12
Peter Doig
White Canoe
1992
Oil on canvas
200.5 x 242.8 cm
(PD253)
Courtesy of Victoria
Miro Gallery

The Group of Seven: first stirrings

The future Group of Seven may have had a very clear agenda, but it took a while to get the pieces to fit. Thomson's death and the First World War were potent interruptions. This 'artistic revolution' followed a familiar modernist pattern, albeit with particular local associations. There was no shortage of painters in Canada, some very skilled, but they were behind the times. The reigning styles favoured by Canadian artists were still those of the Barbizon School or the Hague School, with just a touch of Impressionism. In other words, their work was forty or fifty years out of date. The artists who were to become the Group of Seven – MacDonald, Harris, Jackson, Johnston, Lismer, Varley and Carmichael – along with Thomson, were not flaming revolutionaries eager to embrace the latest fad, but they were impassioned and well-informed, and they saw it as their mission to drag Canadian painting into the modern era.

Both Varley and Lismer trained at art school in Sheffield, while Durham-born MacDonald spent several years in London working as a commercial artist. Harris studied painting for three years under Franz Skarbina (1849–1910, co-founder of the Group of Eleven and of the Berlin Secession) in Berlin. A.Y. Jackson studied at the Académie Julien in Paris, and Franklin Carmichael also studied briefly in Antwerp before war intervened. Jackson and Varley were both war artists, recording the horrors of the Western Front alongside Paul Nash and Augustus John under the auspices of Lord Beaverbrook's Canadian War Memorials Fund (Lismer was also a war artist, but based back in Canada), and exhibiting with them at the great Royal Academy exhibition of the Fund's work in 1919. Frank Johnston (his full name was Francis Hans Johnston – he eventually opted for Franz) studied in Philadelphia at the Pennsylvania Academy, whence so many of the influential American 'Ash Can' school emerged. In fact, Thomson was by far the least trained artist among them, but he learned much from his association with his better-schooled friends. Meeting and sharing studio space with Jackson early in 1914 was clearly a formative experience

for him, and several of his trips into Algonquin Park were in the company of other artists, Lismer, Jackson and Varley among them.

Meanwhile, Lawren Harris and Jim MacDonald had shared a transformative experience in 1913 when they visited the Scandinavian Art exhibition held that year in Buffalo, discovering, for the first time, a 'northern' school of painting that had its own language expressing a profound relationship with the empty wastes of the Scandinavian wilderness. Some of Harris's own paintings from that period are effectively exercises in the bold and profoundly decorative style of the Swede Gustav Fjaestad (fig. 38, p. 49). Indeed, some of Thomson's more decorative works, and some of his winter pieces, also reflect a passing interest in what he had probably heard about Scandinavian painting from Harris or MacDonald, or seen at second-hand in their work. There is, interestingly enough, no evidence that any of the artists travelled to New York for the famous Armory show of 1913 (although Harris at least could certainly have afforded to do so), where they would have seen some of the most advanced work that Europe had to offer, by Matisse, Picasso and Duchamp. It was, quite possibly, simply of no interest to them.

There was supposedly no leader of the Group, but it is clear that the driving force behind the gradual coming-together of like-minded artists that happened in the decade before the Group of Seven's formal creation in 1920 was Harris. All of the other artists had to struggle, at least initially, living a more or less hand-to-mouth existence. Most of them worked as commercial artists, although Lismer, Johnston, MacDonald and Varley all took up teaching as a way to bolster their income. Harris was different. He was independently wealthy, one of the heirs to the Massey-Harris family business – then the largest manufacturer of farm machinery in the world. He had the leisure time to theorise and plan; he never directly bankrolled his artist colleagues, but he facilitated their endeavours in other ways, including purchasing work.

Fig. 13
**Arthur Lismer
and Tom Thomson
in canoe, Canoe Lake,
Algonquin Park**
May 1914
McMichael
Canadian Art
Collection Archives

Leading or following?

Early on, Harris articulated the need for a new Canadian style of painting, and started manoeuvring to bring it about. With the support of wealthy Toronto ophthalmologist Dr James MacCallum, another important figure and early patron of the future group members, he built a studio to provide a kind of home for many of the artists (it still stands, in the Rosedale district of Toronto, although it is now converted for residential use). Furthermore Harris worked hard, with MacCallum's help, to entice Jackson, whose experience and skills were highly advanced but who worked in Montreal, to Toronto – and to keep him there, when he contemplated moving to New York. It seems as if Harris viewed Jackson as a potential leader, or at least catalyst, for the new 'Algonquin School', as this early informal grouping of painters was sometimes known.

In 1913, a definite campaign to 'land' Jackson was played out. In March there was correspondence between MacDonald and Jackson (in Montreal), introducing Harris as the would-be buyer of a Jackson canvas from 1910, *Edge of the Maple Wood*, which Harris had long admired. Jackson was delighted to sell him the canvas; he was frustrated with the Montreal art scene, and a trip to Toronto ensued, followed by a visit to Georgian Bay on Lake Huron. At the end of the summer, Jackson stayed on to paint in a rented cottage. Harris then produced his trump card: he urged Dr MacCallum to call on the Montreal artist. MacCallum offered Jackson the use of his own, much more comfortable and somewhat more weatherproof, cottage on the island he owned in Go Home Bay (also in Georgian Bay), where Jackson stayed until the end of October. More importantly, Dr MacCallum made him a fantastic offer: if he would come to Toronto and work in the studio building, he, MacCallum, would guarantee buying sufficient pictures to keep him going for a year (he was soon to make the same offer successfully to Thomson). Jackson stayed. It was as if Harris was arranging his chess pieces for the launch of a grand endeavour. The year 1914 saw the opening of the studio building and considerable fraternal group activity, including a moment in October when not only Thomson, but also Jackson, Varley and Lismer were all in Algonquin Park at the same time, sketching together (fig. 13).

But by then war had been declared;[17] if Harris had hoped to make something more formal out of this group of artist friends, the timing was out of joint; and by the end of that year, something else unexpected had happened. Whatever role Jackson had been led to expect to play in the new grouping of artists – and one possible role was probably conceived by Harris to be a kind of mentor to Thomson – he was taken by surprise in Algonquin Park that autumn. In a letter to MacDonald, we can almost hear Jackson dismantling preconceptions: 'Tom is doing some exciting stuff … He keeps one up to time. Very often I have to figure out if I am leading or following'.[18] Clearly, his expectation had been that he would lead, but the blue touch-paper on Thomson's talent had been lit in the meantime, probably to a large degree by Jackson himself, and witnessing the flare briefly at first hand, he was man and artist enough to acknowledge it.

In June 1915, Jackson enlisted in the 60th battalion and left for Europe, where more than 60,000 fellow Canadians were to die in the war. By the time he returned, Thomson was dead too; but Jackson quickly acquainted himself with what his friend had achieved in his absence, and was instrumental in organising the first memorial exhibition of his work, in Montreal, in March 1919. Thomson's work seemed to all of the future Group to provide an exemplar of what they were searching for: a true 'Canadian' voice. It was to be one of the most important catalysts for what followed, and the trajectory of the Group of Seven was like the ripples spreading outwards, geographically and spiritually, from Canoe Lake and those three extraordinary years of Thomson's creative intensity.

Algoma arabesque

Jackson and Varley witnessed the carnage of war in Europe at first hand (Jackson was wounded at Ypres), and painted it under the auspices of the Canadian War Memorials Fund.[19] Lismer was by then Principal of the Victoria School of Art and Design in Halifax, Nova Scotia, and also did some painting of minesweepers and Halifax harbour for

Fig. 14
**A.Y. Jackson,
Frank Johnston
and Lawren
Harris on the
Algoma boxcar**
McMichael
Canadian Art
Collection Archives

the Fund. In 1916, Lawren Harris had enlisted as an instructor in musketry at Toronto and Camp Borden but was to receive a medical discharge from the army in May 1918, having suffered a breakdown. He immediately turned to art again as therapy, and went exploring with Dr MacCallum, taking the Algoma Central Railway northwards. He was impressed enough by what he saw to quickly organise a second trip, this time with MacDonald and Johnston joining him and Dr MacCallum. Travelling up the Algoma railway, they were much taken with the potential of what they saw – the rocks, waterfalls, and trees of this new landscape. It was understandable that the artists wanted to find an alternative to Algonquin Park so soon after Thomson's death. Jackson spoke for all, writing from the turmoil of the war in Europe: 'without Tom the north country seems a desolation of bush and rock'.[20] Algoma would then provide another great source of inspiration and the impetus for the creation of the Group of Seven. An exhibition of Algoma work from that autumn by MacDonald, Harris and Johnston was held at the Art Museum of Toronto in April 1919, although MacDonald had already shown some Algoma subjects at the Ontario Society of Artists (OSA) exhibition in March, including *The Little Falls* (cat. 66). The critical response was encouraging, though as usual not matched by sales (this was a regular problem throughout the Group's life).

A third trip took place in September 1919, and this time Jackson, back from the war and having spent August at his beloved Georgian Bay, was available to come too. They travelled in some style, thanks to Harris, who had fitted out a special boxcar as a kind of travelling studio (see fig. 14). The weather was wet, so the comforts of the boxcar were much appreciated – at least by Jackson. He recorded that '[t]he other chaps are all out sketching under umbrellas. They are all trying to turn out four a day, and can't stop if it rains. MacDonald and Johnston are Christian Scientists and Harris a theosophist, and they don't see much difference between rain and sunshine'.[21] Jackson's wry observation confirms that there was more than just artistic fervour at work.

The Group of Seven

The success of the 1919 exhibition of Algoma work had perhaps clarified something for the Group. The most negative critical reaction to their work thus far had occurred in the context of much broader exhibitions at the Royal Canadian Academy or the OSA. While all the artists continued to send work to these exhibitions, it was clear that they were polarised when exhibited alongside the more academic artists – they were easy targets for reactionary critics. It followed that the time might finally have arrived to create a different context for themselves, one in which they were seen as a cohesive movement, rather than as the reverse side of someone else's coin. Plans were therefore laid for an exhibition in May 1920 at the Art Gallery of Toronto, to involve the core group plus a couple of 'invited' artists.

In March that year a more formal coming-together occurred: no less than the long-delayed formation of the Group of Seven, at Harris's mansion at 63 Queen's Park, Toronto (now the site of St Michael's College, University of Toronto). All of the initial seven members were present, except Jackson, who was away painting on Georgian Bay. It had been decided that this was not to be a grand secession from the established societies and forums already existing in Toronto – no one wished to antagonise the Academy or the OSA. So this was not to be a new Society, merely a cooperative Group, with no leaders or formal proceedings. In many ways it was simply a pragmatic alliance for facilitating exhibitions, starting with the first Group of Seven show in May 1920; no single person would choose what was displayed, one of the artists would design a poster (the first was by Johnston, while Carmichael designed the catalogue). There was a kitty, though no treasurer – fifteen percent commission from any sales would go towards costs. Text was provided on the first occasion by Barker Fairley – almost the eighth member of the Group, another Yorkshireman, and a great supporter. They even had a logo, again designed by Carmichael.

That first exhibition included 121 catalogued works; fifty-four canvases, forty-four oil sketches, sixteen temperas by Johnston. In the end the 'invited guests' accounted for only seven pictures.

Fig. 15
Frank Johnston
Serenity, Lake
of the Woods (detail)
1922
Oil on canvas
102.3 × 128.4 cm
Collection of the
Winnipeg Art
Gallery (L-102)

The paintings were not all Algoma landscapes; they included some done for the War Records. Both Varley and Harris provided portraits; Harris included some of his urban subjects; and the landscapes covered a fair amount of geography, including views of Halifax harbour and Nova Scotia, alongside a couple of Georgian Bay pictures by Jackson. Sales were rather miserable: three to private buyers, three to the National Gallery. But Eric Brown, the National Gallery's Director, did something of more tangible use by organising the exhibition as a touring show, removing only those that had been painted on commission (such as Varley's portraits) and adding four pictures by Thomson. This meant that the first Group of Seven show was seen in the States, first of all at the Worcester Art Museum, then travelling on to Boston, Rochester, Toledo, Detroit, Cleveland, Buffalo, Columbus, Minneapolis and Muskegon, Michigan.

Seven minus one

The issue of sales (or rather the lack of them) was to cause the first upset almost immediately. Frank Johnston was a prolific painter, whose work in tempera always seemed slightly out of place among work by the other Group members. It was more decorative and more immediately attractive to many viewers; it also sold better. Not at the first Group of Seven exhibition, however. In the same year, in December, he was able to mount an impressive display of 200 of his own works in a solo show at a department store gallery in Toronto (T. Eaton Co.) and sales were good. He decided that association with the Group of Seven would have a negative effect on his capacity to sell paintings; he would do better on his own.[22] So no sooner had the Group of Seven formed than they were one down. When the second Group of Seven show opened on 7 May 1921, they were in fact to all intents and purposes a group of six. Johnston had left for Winnipeg, having accepted the post of Principal of the School of Art there. It is from Winnipeg that his beautiful picture, *Serenity, Lake of the Woods*, comes (fig. 15, cat. 64), illustrating Johnston's exceptional skills as a landscapist, but also clearly underlining his essential difference of approach. It is here paired

with its sketch (cat. 63). By 1924, when he returned to Toronto to teach at the Ontario College of Art, any formal relationship with the Group had ended.

This second exhibition was smaller, comprising forty-eight canvases and forty-one sketches. One of the hits of the show was Varley's *Stormy Weather, Georgian Bay* (cat. 52). This is one of the Group of Seven's most triumphant masterpieces, an astonishingly bravura evocation of wind, sun, water and air from an artist who was already beginning to focus mainly on portraiture. It sold to the National Gallery of Canada, along with a couple of Jacksons and a Carmichael. There were no other sales. *Stormy Weather* was something of a spectacular exception in Varley's career. He was by nature a portraitist, Canada's finest in fact, but his landscapes regularly display an exceptional quality, with a very individual sense of colour and form. His rather rackety personal life and periods of extreme hardship led to his being seen as the wild man of the Group. He moved to Vancouver to teach at the School of Decorative and Applied Arts in 1926, and from his period in British Columbia came a series of magical landscape images (cats. 98–102). However, his departure inevitably distanced him from the Group.

Man, nature, spirit: North Shore, Lake Superior

Harris and Jackson seem to have been prime movers behind one of the defining ideas of the Group, the sense that the 'new' Canadian artist must not only survive in the wilderness but also cover as much ground as possible. Eventually, these artists recorded not only the landscapes of the Canadian Shield, but the Arctic, the Rockies, the West Coast and Newfoundland as well, with much in between.

At the outset, however, Jackson, Harris and Lismer remained enthralled by Algoma. In 1920 (even as the first Group of Seven show was still on) they had headed off to Mongoose Lake there; and in May 1921, the three of them went to camp on the Agawa River and Montreal Lake. But, although the trio visited the district again in the autumn, this time to Sand Lake, the loyalty of at least one of the artists was flagging. As Jackson was to put it:

'The Algoma country was too opulent for Harris; he wanted something bare and stark'.[23] When Lismer returned to Toronto to resume his teaching duties, Jackson and Harris headed by train further along the north shore of Lake Superior, where Harris was to find one of his great subjects, and begin to refine his own personal style (cats. 107 –113). This landscape was indeed bare and stark, having been burned over some years before. New growth had not yet had time to establish itself. Fire had erased the surfeit of detail that had begun to irk Harris in Algoma, and revealed the 'bones' beneath the landscape. It led to a new simplification and austerity in his work – what natural forces had done to the landscape of the north shore, Harris would increasingly do to his own imagery – stripping down the forms of the landscape to express what he saw as its spiritual power.

This search for the spiritual was completely characteristic of Harris, who was a theosophist. The Theosophical Society was at the peak of its popularity in North America in the 1920s, and its overarching objectives of universal brotherhood, the study of comparative religion and the spiritual understanding of Nature appealed to many artists and musicians. Harris was a natural-born seeker after Truth: he talked about human creativity in quasi-religious terms: 'Our spirits emerge into purer creative work wherein they change the outward aspect of nature, alter colours, intensify forms, purge rhythms of pettiness, and seek to enable the soul to live in the grand way of certain wondrous moments in the North when the outward aspect of nature becomes for a while full luminous to her informing spirit – and man, nature and spirit are one'.[24] The spiritual search for a deeper immersion in creativity led him ultimately to abstraction, but it is the represent-ational work he completed on the journey towards abstraction that constitutes Harris's most particular contribution to the story of the Group of Seven, and makes him, to many, the most important of the Group.

Meanwhile, the Group of Seven exhibitions carried on. The third exhibition took place in May 1922, with sixty canvases although no sketches this time. Harris, Jackson and Lismer again had the most to show, as a result of their excursions to Algoma. However, MacDonald had a good range of work to exhibit, including *October Shower Gleam*. The sketch for this painting is one of the most startling produced by a Group artist, a lyrical masterpiece of expressionist intensity (cats. 77 and 78). The annual exhibitions, and the Group of Seven itself, had quickly become an accepted part of Toronto cultural life, no longer prompting extravagant criticism in the press. But this year there were no sales at all. The next Group of Seven show would not happen until 1925, after the success of the first British Empire Exhibition at Wembley. All four remaining Group of Seven shows (1926, 1928, 1930 and 1931) repeated the pattern: growing acceptance and acknowledgement, growing numbers of 'invited' contributors, but this acceptance was never to be matched with sales.

The year 1923 saw Jackson painting in Baie-Saint-Paul in March (he generally preferred to spend his winters in Quebec), then back to his happy hunting ground in Georgian Bay; with Harris he travelled in August to Jasper, Alberta, in the Canadian Rockies, where they painted Maligne Lake and the Tonquin Valley. Instead of a Toronto Group of Seven exhibition, Eric Brown put together another touring show of *Modern Canadian Painting* for the States (Minneapolis, Kansas City, Milwaukee, Providence, Worcester and Brooklyn). By the time that show finished its tour in August 1924, to a rather underwhelming response, the first London show at Wembley had finally brought some international recognition and encouragement.

Mountain mad

Meanwhile, MacDonald, in late summer 1924, managed to undertake his first proper sketching trip for a good while, to Lake O'Hara in the Rockies. Jackson and Harris, indefatigable travellers both, would soon follow him. The Rockies were to provide another regular source of inspiration for both MacDonald and Harris in the second half of the 1920s (cats. 88–97 and 117–113).

The immediate result of this was noted humorously by the critic of the *Star Weekly*'s reaction to the Group's 1925 show, who enthused

Fig. 16 (top)
Franklin Carmichael
North Shore,
Lake Superior
1927
Oil on canvas
101.5 x 121.7 cm
The Montreal Museum
of Fine Arts
Purchase, Robert Lindsay Fund

Fig. 17 (bottom)
Alfred Joseph Casson
The White Pine
c. 1957
Oil on canvas
McMichael Canadian Art
Collection, Kleinburg,
Canada, gift of the Founders,
Robert and Signe McMichael
(1966.16.119)

that the painters 'have been successively, and generally successfully, house-haunted, tree-mad, lake-lunatic, river-ridden, birch-bedlamed, aspen-addled, and rock-cracked. This year they are mountain mad'.[25] Other critics, including Barker Fairley, noted, with some concern, the ever-increasing austerity which appeared to be taking Harris in a different direction from his colleagues. Meanwhile, even Franklin Carmichael, always the most decorative and accessible of the Group since Johnston's departure, made the trip to Lake Superior this year with Harris and Jackson, and caught the austerity bug, producing, for the 1926 show, a grimmer and more powerful vision. This landscape was to inspire some of his most beautiful accomplished work (fig. 16).

The year 1926 saw the publication of F.B. Housser's *A Canadian Art Movement: The Story of the Group of Seven*, which ended with the expression of an exalted hope that eventually the rest of the world would look to Canada for artistic inspiration. No doubt the Group's success in London prompted this wild optimism, although Housser was quick to point out that even at Wembley the modernists provided only a fraction of the Canadian paintings on show. In 1926 there had never actually been an exhibition devoted solely to the Group of Seven outside North America (and as far as Britain is concerned, that has remained true up until the present exhibition).

The year also provided a seventh member of the Group again, filling the gap left long before by Johnston's departure. A.J. Casson (1898–1992) provided the decorative element that Carmichael's introduction to the starkness of Lake Superior may have appeared to have chased away. A close colleague of Carmichael, whose assistant he was at Rous & Mann, Casson's take on the Canadian landscape is always hugely attractive and technically adept, while steering clear of any rough edges. As one critic of the 1926 show, perhaps more astutely than he intended, put it: his canvases 'will form resting places for those visitors to the present show who cannot understand Lawren Harris'.[26] More even than Carmichael, Casson's work suggests a designer's sensibility, often with luminous and gorgeous results (fig. 17). It cannot

Fig. 18
**A.Y. Jackson
in the Arctic**
1927
McMichael
Canadian Art
Collection Archives

Fig. 19
**Lawren Harris,
A.Y. Jackson
and Captain
Falke aboard
the Beothic**
1930
Private collection

be said, however, that Casson added anything particularly new or challenging to the mix – indeed he was eventually to be elected President of the Academy. In the years to come, two more artists, Edwin Holgate (1892–1977) from Montreal and, right at the end, Lionel LeMoine Fitzgerald (1890–1956) from Winnipeg, were invited to join as well. The Group of Seven seems rarely to have numbered seven.

The Arctic

The final frontier for the Group was reached in 1927 when Jackson went to the Arctic (fig. 18). It had not passed unnoticed that the Group were spreading ever further afield. Jackson managed to interest the Minister of the Interior in a proposal that he, Jackson, should paint the most northerly point in the country and present the resulting painting to the Department. A voyage was duly set up for him, departing in July 1927, in the steamer *Beothic*, which normally took supplies to Royal Canadian Mounted Police outposts in the Arctic. At the Bache Peninsula on Ellesmere Island, he made a sketch for his promised painting. Clearly having relished the adventure and dangers of the journey, he made it back home in September, with material for several canvases and a book of drawings. The next year, in July 1928, he headed north again, to Great Slave Lake in the Western Canadian Arctic – an area little known then, although the discovery of gold in 1930 was to change that.

Another invitation from the Government for an artistic Arctic voyage came in 1930, this time for Jackson and Harris together, again on the *Beothic* and following the same route as in 1927 (fig. 19). The two artists went ashore whenever it was possible, making sketches that they then worked up on panels or boards back in their cabin on board. In Lancaster Sound, they encountered 'the wrecks of old ice floes, worn into all kinds of fantastic forms and unbelievably blue in colour'.[27] In the Hudson Strait, at Lake Harbour, Harris found material for some fine paintings. Indeed, according to Jackson, on this trip his friend had made 'enough studies to keep himself busy for the next two years'.[28] Harris was born to paint icebergs (cats. 121–124).

The last Group of Seven show, their eighth, was held in December 1931. By this time the shows had to be bolstered with work by invited guests, whose work often outnumbered contributions from the Group itself – most of the Group were widely scattered and engaged in other projects. MacDonald, although he still managed to spend time during the summer up in the Rockies, had always struggled financially and had been pleased to accept the role of Principal of the Ontario School of Art in 1927. He was not only the oldest of the Group, but also the most frail. He died after a stroke in 1932, aged only fifty-nine, and the next year the Group decided to disband. They had never been a formal society, had no officers, little if any money, but in terms of recognition and reputation their mission had been achieved. Modernism in Canada had been addressed; they were established, and accepted. Out of the ashes of the Group of Seven arose another group, the Canadian Group of Painters, to which many of the surviving Seven also belonged. None of them had yet earned much money from their painting, and in 1933 it is probable that they can have had little inkling how famous they would in time become in their own country.

Rarely, in fact, have the objectives of a group of painters been so resoundingly achieved. The Group of Seven effectively taught Canadians how to 'see' their country; their vision of Canada is rooted deep in the Canadian psyche to this day. It was a great national achievement – perhaps greater than even they could have been aware – and one that deserves to be more widely appreciated outside Canada. Six of the ten artists who were members of the Group are buried in the beautiful grounds of the McMichael Canadian Art Collection at Kleinburg, Ontario, forming a kind of national shrine, very close to Tom Thomson's painting shack. One thing is certain, however – Tom Thomson would be spinning in his grave (wherever that might be) to know how much the sketches he used to give away now achieve at auction.[29]

Notes

1 A reference to Percy Wyndham Lewis, 'Canadian nature and its painters', *The Listener*, vol. XXXVI, no. 920, 29 August 1946, pp. 267–68: 'It would be idle to pretend that the oils… produced by Thomson … would set the Thames or the Seine on fire'.

2 Anthony Bertram, 'The Palace of Arts, Wembley', *Saturday Review* (London), 7 June 1924.

3 *Art News*, 31 May 1924.

4 In the *Toronto Daily Star*, January 1925, in Charles C. Hill, *The Group of Seven: Art for a Nation*, exh. cat., National Gallery of Canada, 1995, p. 155.

5 Hector Charlesworth in 'Pictures that can be heard: A survey of the Ontario Society of Artists' Exhibition', *Saturday Night*, vol. XXIX, no. 23, 18 March 1916, pp. 5, 11, referring to J.E.H. MacDonald's painting, *The Elements*.

6 H.F. Gadsby, 'The Hot Mush School or Peter and I', *Toronto Daily Star*, 12 December 1913, p. 6.

7 The MacDonald canvas was displayed in the Barbican's 1991 exhibition 'The True North: Canadian Landscape Painting 1896–1939'; catalogue edited and with an introduction by Michael Tooby, Lund Humphries, in association with Barbican Art Gallery, London, 1991.

8 Foreword, *Exhibition of Canadian Art*, 26 November–23 December 1925, exh. cat., Whitechapel Art Gallery, 1925.

9 Augustus John made this reference in his introduction to an exhibition of Innes's work at the Graves Art Gallery, Sheffield, in 1961; quoted in Michael Holroyd, *Augustus John*, Vintage, 1997, p. 353.

10 F.B. Housser, *A Canadian Art Movement: The Story of the Group of Seven*, MacMillan, 1926.

11 Housser, p. 11.

12 This is actually wrong on both counts. Thomson was buried at Leith, and born in Claremont.

13 A.Y. Jackson, *A Painter's Country, the autobiography of A.Y. Jackson*, Clarke, Irwin & Co. Ltd, Toronto, 1958, p. 56.

14 Housser, p. 15.

15 The most recent and most exhaustive discussion of Thomson's death can be found in Roy MacGregor's *Northern Light*, Vintage Books, 2010.

16 This is certainly the belief of Roy MacGregor, based on forensic reconstruction methods applied to photographs of a skull dug up in the Canoe Lake cemetery in the 1950s.

17 Great Britain declared war on Germany on 4 August 1914.

18 A.Y. Jackson to J.E.H. MacDonald, 5 October 1914. National Archives of Canada, Ottawa, MG30 D111, vol. 1, correspondence 1914–24, quoted by Charles Hill in *Tom Thomson*, exh. cat., Art Gallery of Ontario and National Gallery of Canada, 2002, p. 126.

19 Set up by Max Aitken, Lord Beaverbrook, in Autumn 1916 as a means of recording the Canadian contribution to the war, originally employing British artists only, but eventually signing up Jackson, Lismer and Varley.

20 Jackson to MacDonald from Shoreham, England, 4 August 1917, copy in the McMichael Collection, Kleinburg, Ontario; MacDonald papers.

21 Jackson, postmarked Franz, Ont. to Florence Clement, Waterloo, Ont., 29 Sept. 1919, The Naomi Jackson Groves fonds, Library and Archives Canada, M930 – D351, quoted in Hill, *The Group of Seven: Art for a Nation*, exh. cat., National Gallery of Canada, Ottawa, 1995.

22 Although Johnston had a very successful career, it is as a founder member of the Group of Seven that he is famous.

23 Jackson, *A Painter's Country*, p. 57.

24 Bess Harris and R.G.P. Colgrove, *Lawren Harris*, MacMillan, Toronto, 1969, p. 61.

25 Augustus Bridle, '"School of Seven" exhibit is riot of impressions', *Toronto Star Weekly*, 10 January 1925, quoted in Hill, *The Group of Seven: Art for a Nation*, p. 157.

26 Fred Jacob, 'New member is added to the Group of Seven', *Toronto Mail and Empire*, 8 May 1926, quoted in Hill, *The Group of Seven: Art for a Nation*, p. 199.

27 Ibid., p. 131.

28 Ibid., p. 135.

29 At Heffel Fine Art Auction House in Toronto, 26 November 2009, Tom Thomson's sketch *Early Spring, Canoe Lake* fetched $2,749,500.

Landscape Atomysticism
A Revelation of Tom Thomson

Anna Hudson

Fig. 20
Tom Thomson
Northern Lights (detail)
1916 or 1917
Oil on wood
21.5 x 26.7 cm
National Gallery of Canada, Ottawa,
bequest of Dr J.M. MacCallum,
Toronto, 1944 (4677r)

Tom Thomson sat watching as the sky deepened into night. He was studying the evening skies over Algonquin Park, intent on archiving their signature colour harmonies during the late autumn and early spring – when the mosquitoes and black flies were gone. One cold wintry night he made a discovery. The snowy shoreline and icy lake water began to glow, and an aurora borealis shot lightning flares past barely twinkling stars. As he sat, transfixed by the energy the earth seemed to radiate, he brushed in an analogous colour harmony of purples and blues, and roughed out the topographic bones of the scene, including a shadowy bank of trees. Up along the arching silhouette of the distant hillside, he pulled in an acidic green, capturing the spectral light of oxygen discharging its excess electrical energy. Thomson's *Northern Lights* (cat. 34) visualises the new world order of the atomic age that began with the discoveries of relativity and quantum. Almost a century later the sketch remains as provocative as ever. This electrified landscape is a haunting reminder of a reality beyond empirical reach, as mysterious as the death of the artist himself less than three months later.

The drive toward a world in which 'one can, in principle, master all things by calculation', described by the German social theorist Max Weber in 1919, faltered amidst the chaos of World War One.[1] The call to order of an industrialised and rationalised society, essential for the development of modern nations, had boiled over with dissent between states. Within them populations savoured the ability to express their individuality through capitalist consumer culture, not yet sceptical of its exploitative power. From Weber's perspective the experience of modernity in the early twentieth century can be summarised by the tension between individual autonomy and collective order. In retrospect this tension looks like an irresolvable contradiction. The ever enigmatic Tom Thomson serves as a case in point; his oil sketches and canvases produced over the five short years of his career remain fresh and inspiring visions of nature because they never settle into a landscape convention. Instead Thomson sought out visual contradictions in the landscape and locked them in compositional tension. Their effect encapsulates the epistemological crisis that accompanied two major discoveries of modern physics: quantum and the theory of relativity. Both proposed an ultimately unknowable world, replete with mystery.

Thomson's extended sojourns to Algonquin National Park fit neatly with a popular ideal of *mens sana in corpore sano* (a sound mind in a sound body), revived in the late nineteenth century along with the Olympics. From this emerged 'physical culture', a catchphrase for men's self-improvement in Europe (especially Germany). In Britain and North America it built on Victorian muscular Christianity and Thomas Carlyle's cult of manliness.[2] The Young Men's Christian Association (YMCA) encouraged Canadian men to associate a strong and healthy constitution with empowerment. Thomson, the man, is still bathed by the glowing appeal of perfect health and beauty promoted by physical culture and utopian life reform movements.[3] He is remembered as an outdoorsman, profoundly attuned to nature. While it is tempting to dismiss this romantic legacy as naïve, it is indicative of the spiritual crisis that accompanied World War One, and which arguably continues to underwrite scientific inquiry into our collective perception of reality. As explained by Mircea Eliade, modern secular life, with its linear thread of progress, threatened to erase any vestige of sacred time.[4] This is precisely what inspired so many early twentieth-century artists in the West to seek out the primal, and to imagine the sacred space/time of ritual.

Thomson's return to the so-called wilderness exemplified this trend, a fact that has proven disturbing for historians of Canadian art. At issue in the context of Canada's colonial history is whether the canoe-paddling Thomson was a white man *gone native*, like the Englishman, Archibald Belaney, who deceptively styled himself as 'Grey Owl'. With increasing recognition of the fact that European settlement of Aboriginal territory meant that hundreds of thousands of indigenous peoples lost their lives and livelihoods, any trope of *Indianness* has become suspicious, particularly the idea of innate knowledge of nature. To underscore the tragicomedy of it all, Algonquin Park was in fact 'a highly controlled space with a significant industrial history' rendering it far from 'pristine wilderness'.[5] The road to recovery of Thomson and the Group of Seven from their damaging association with Canada's tourism industry and resource-based national economy is long and painful for many academics, who struggle with the artists' romanticised wilderness appeal. Revisionist historians of Canadian art struggle still to dislodge the canonical predominance of the white male wilderness painter, whose heroic landscapes signal the collusion of capital and political power that erased First Peoples from the map of Canada.[6] As current environmental debates about climate change indicate, however, our collective relationship with nature is still richly imagined, if contradictory. Thomson's representations of Algonquin Park are like campfire stories, around which we bond under the night sky. Even our ecological anxiety cannot dislodge their draw.

The war played a significant role in defining Thomson 'within the culture of mourning and an emerging national identity that became so powerful in the years following his death', argues Andrew Hunter.[7] 'In death', he explains, 'soldiers made the land sacred, just as Thomson made Algonquin Park hallowed ground'.[8] Certainly Thomson came to personify Canada in a manner comparable to Marianne, the personification of France violated by war. Thomson's paintings then fell into the service of English-Canadian national identity, especially *The West Wind* (figs. 21 and 22) of 1917, an image which has since been widely reproduced and disseminated. The struggling pine, centred in the composition, begs to be read as a figure, a sacrificial soldier, and even a reference to the artist himself as a double for Canada. But what if one rejects the symbolic, politicised reading of this painting to consider instead its compositional structure and formal elements? To do so would be to encounter this Canadian icon anew.

Fig. 21
Tom Thomson
Sketch for The
West Wind
1916
Oil on composite
wood board
21.4 x 26.8 cm
Art Gallery of
Ontario, Toronto,
gift from the J.S.
McLean Collection,
Toronto, 1969,
donated by the
Ontario Heritage
Foundation,
1988 (I.69.49)

Fig. 22
Tom Thomson
The West Wind
Winter 1916–17
Oil on canvas
120.7 x 137.9 cm
Art Gallery of
Ontario, Toronto,
gift of the Canadian
Club of Toronto,
1926 (784)

A comparison of the sketch and canvas of *The West Wind* demonstrates how laboured Thomson's canvases appear. This criticism has been explained as the result of his lack of expertise in relation, for example, to Fred Varley, the consummate painter amongst the Group of Seven. In his sketch for *The West Wind* the paint application is uniformly bold and opaque. A visual continuum of repeating colour and pattern flows through the sky, water, and land, which are separated by strategic gaps of pigment. Bare board accents the horizon and contours the foreground pine. The tree appears to glow; it has an aura. I have always been intrigued to compare how Thomson and the members of the Group of Seven, especially Lawren Harris, reproduced the aura-like effect of unpainted board in their canvases by outlining the landscape features, especially the trees, in orangey-brown pigment.

This unusual practice of evoking auras can be explained in Harris's case as an expression of his turn-of-the century spiritualism – and theosophy in particular – through which he envisioned aesthetic experience as the recognition of the secrets of a cosmic universal 'oneness' of being. Harris abandoned representation by the mid-1930s to hone, like Piet Mondrian, a more purely theosophical visual language. Notably the earliest writers on Thomson – Blodwen Davies and Fred Housser – being Theosophists themselves – read spirituality into his paintings.[9] I cannot help but wonder if Thomson's radiating contour outlines are less spiritual auras than responses to the spectral signatures of elements radiating their excess energy. His powers of observation were not only acute, but scientific. By 1917 Thomson was calling his sketches 'records,'[10] given that they functioned as data-filled documentation of nature. His uncle, Dr William Brodie, was a well-known naturalist, with 'the eye of the scientist and of the artist', whose extensive collection of specimens was internationally recognised. He encouraged expansive scientific thinking about the dynamism of life, drawing on Western and Eastern philosophical traditions, and rethinking Charles Darwin's theory of natural selection 'within a universal, even mystical context'.[11] Would this familial background account for *The West Wind* being such a discordant painting? By comparison to the uniformly styled sketch, the sky has become fluid and luminous, the water choppy and viscous, the foreground rock massive and magnified with lichen, and the pine tree an elegant study of tensile strength. In other words, the character of each landscape feature was well preserved as an accounting of its elemental make-up. Thomson's canvas can thus be read as a compelling reworking of a nineteenth-century botanical study into a kind of visualised periodic table.

The epistemological crisis of modernity caused by confusion over what is knowable, quantifiable, and ultimately controllable, intensified during the time Thomson was painting in Algonquin. While World War One was its most obvious catalyst, given the scale of both its industrial progress and human loss, two key discoveries in theoretical physics redrew the relationship of science, religion, and philosophy which, since the Renaissance, had evolved into separate fields of inquiry into the nature of reality. The rigid authority of experience, of empirical fact, that hardened natural science during the nineteenth century rested on the concepts of classical physics, space, time, matter and causality. 'The progress of science was pictured as a crusade of conquest into the material world'. As Albert Einstein explained, this simple and synoptic image of the surrounding world was exchanged for another as a result of his own General Theory of Relativity (completed in 1915), along with ongoing research into quantum energy following Max Planck's proposition of its existence in 1900. Theoretical physics in the first two decades of the twentieth century provided instead a 'world-picture' more closely corresponding to 'what the poet does, and the painter, and the speculative philosopher, each in his own way'.[12] Empiricism,

as Einstein reflected, could not underwrite the advanced theoretical physics of his day. A realignment of perspectives on reality emerged from what Werner Heisenberg subsequently described as the Uncertainty Principle (1927),[13] outlining the limits of scientific method to rationalise space and time at the atomic level, specifically regarding its ability to chart any continuous motion of electrons around the nucleus.[14] The confidence in the scientific method and in rational thinking to replace 'all other safeguards of the human mind' collapsed.[15] While Einstein still believed, as had classical physicists since Newton, that 'the supreme task of the physicist is the discovery of the most general elementary laws from which the world-picture can be deduced', logic had been dislodged by intuition, 'a feeling for the order lying behind the appearance' – an *Einfühlung*.[16] 'Atomysticism' was how Heisenberg remembered the strange elusiveness of the nature of reality debated most intensely during the 1920s. 'Einstein keeps talking about God', recalled Heisenberg. And '[f]rom some of Planck's utterances it would seem that he sees no contradiction between religion and science, indeed that he believes the two are perfectly compatible'.[17]

Coincident with the war, and in tandem with the theoretical foundations of quantum mechanics, an international literary and scientific community embraced conflict and contradiction as the wellspring of new knowledge. Among its most influential proponents was Rabindranath Tagore, the Bengali writer and musician (and winner of the 1913 Nobel Prize for Literature), who toured the globe lecturing on the dangers of nationalism and consumerism. He shared with Einstein an acceptance of a paradox: being that the scientific observation of reality ultimately reveals the human mind to itself, and is thus subjective.[18] 'Art', he commented on his 1929 visit to Canada, comparably 'represents man's personal world of reality in which he is revealed to himself in his own light, the light that has its numerous rays of emotion, visible and invisible'.[19] At the height of his popularity in 1916–17, during a tour to Japan and the United States, Tagore led 'the most popular philosophic thing in Europe today', as one journalist surmised, 'a restoration of God and the soul in terms of biology or of mysticism'.[20] In his poetry, as in Thomson's paintings, Tagore locked contradictory landscape imagery in compositional tension:

> *Here rolls the sea*
> *And even here*
> *Lies the other shore*
> *Waiting to be reached*
> *Yes here*
> *Is the everlasting present*
> *Not distant*
> *Not anywhere else*[21]

In his autobiography, *My Reminiscences*, which appeared in English in 1917, Tagore described the delight 'of attaining the infinite within the finite'.[22] The feeling he captured of suspended time in indeterminable space perfectly describes the atomic world of quantum, and the cataclysmic revelation that space and time are the limited forms for human perception of transcendental reality and cosmic time.[23] With this revelation comes an appreciation of Thomson's ability to evoke a curious amalgam of joy and pathos, exemplified by the quantum dance of the aurora borealis in *Northern Lights*. That this would characterise Canada, in the end, as a polar country, is less nationalist than scientific. *Northern Lights* visualises the drama of solar wind carrying energy plasma (protons and electrons) to the earth's magnetosphere. Once charged this field erupts in a substorm, releasing excess energy in a spectral display of photons, expressed in waves that sweep across the night sky. Thomson, the artist, sits in the middle of this atomic theatre, witnessing its quantum dynamic on a heavenly scale. The work of art achieves what science could not: it is an empirical record of metaphysical reality.

> *Beware alone of Reason and of Science,*
> *Man's highest powers, unholy in alliance.*
> *You let yourself, through dazzling witchcraft,*
> *yield To all temptations of the Quantum field.*[24]

Notes

1   Max Weber, 'Science as a Vocation', 1919/1946; as quoted in Sung Ho Kim, 'Max Weber', *The Stanford Encyclopedia of Philosophy* (Fall 2008 Edition), Edward N. Zalta, ed., URL = http://plato.stanford.edu/archives/fall2008/entries/weber/

2   The 'muscular Christian' movement, as Donald Hall writes in his introduction, '[associated] physical strength, religious certainty, and the ability to shape and control the world around oneself… [For] muscular Christians, the male body appears as a metaphor for social, national, and religious bodies, while at the same time it attempts to enforce a particular construction of those bodies'. Donald E. Hall, 'Introduction', in Donald E. Hall, ed., *Muscular Christianity: Embodying the Victorian Age*, New York: Cambridge University Press, 1994, pp. 7–8.

3   Supporters of the life reform movement in Germany 'believed that modern civilization, urbanization, and industrialization had alienated human beings from their 'natural' living conditions, leading them down a path of progressive degeneration'. Michael Hau, *The Cult of Health and Beauty in Germany – A Social History*, 1890–1930, Chicago: University of Chicago Press, 2003, p. 1.

4   Mircea Eliade, a controversial religious historian of this period, argues 'the *completely* profane world, the wholly desacralized cosmos, is a recent discovery in the history of the human spirit'. Mircea Eliade, *The Sacred and the Profane: The Nature of Religion*, translated by Willard R. Trask, 1957; New York: Harcourt Brace Jovanovich, 1959, p. 13.

5   Andrew Hunter, 'Mapping Tom', in Dennis Reid, ed., *Tom Thomson*, Toronto and Ottawa: Art Gallery of Ontario and the National Gallery of Canada, 2002, p. 30.

6   Ibid., p. 30.

7   See: Anna Hudson, 'After the Group of Seven', in *The Group of Seven Project, 1920–2005*, Toronto: Ontario Association of Art Galleries, 2010, pp. 20–37. See also: John O'Brian and Peter White, *Beyond Wilderness: The Group of Seven, Canadian Identity, and Contemporary Art*, Montreal/Kingston: McGill-Queen's University Press, 2007.

8   Hunter, 'Mapping Tom', p. 40.

9   Ibid., p. 41.

10   Ibid., p. 41.

11   'He', in reference to Tom Thomson, wrote Housser, 'painted intuitively surrendering to the mood of his environment'. In so doing he could capture 'the spirit of the scene' – 'as though northern nature itself were speaking to you through a perfectly attuned and seasoned medium'. F.B. Housser, *A Canadian Art Movement: The Story of the Group of Seven*, Toronto, 1926, pp. 117, 119. See also: Blodwen Davies, *Tom Thomson: the story of a man who looked for beauty and for truth in the wilderness*, Toronto, Canada: Discus Press, 1935.

12   Joan Murray, *Tom Thomson: The Last Spring*, Toronto: Dundurn Press, 1994, pp. 1–2.

13   Suzanne Zeller, Brodie, William, *Dictionary of Canadian Biography Online*, URL = http://www.biographi.ca/009004-119.01-e.php?BioId=40703&query=

14   Albert Einstein, 'Preface', to Max Planck, *Where is Science Going?*, James Murphy, transl. and ed., Woodbridge, Conn.: Ox Bow Press, 1933/1981, pp. 10–11.

15   Heisenberg's Uncertainty Principle summarised

the impact of the theory of relativity and quantum mechanics on scientific observation of reality, whereby the objective determination of time-space phenomena did not explain atomic structure, most notably quantum leaps of electrons. See: Werner Heisenberg, 'Nobel Lecture: The Development of Quantum Mechanics', 11 December, 1933; reprinted in Werner Heisenberg, *Physics and Philosophy: The Revolution in Modern Science*, New York: Harper Perennial Modern Thought, 1958/2007, pp. 183–201.

16 'Heisenberg had discovered that quantum mechanics forbids, at any given moment, the precise determination of both the position and the momentum of a particle. It is possible to measure exactly either where an electron is or how fast it is moving, but not both simultaneously. It was nature's price for knowing one of the two exactly'. Heisenberg's Uncertainty Principle thus identified a 'quantum dance of give-and-take'. Manjit Kumar, *Quantum – Einstein, Bohr and the Great Debate About the Nature of Reality*, New York: W.W. Norton & Company, 2008, pp. 231–32.

17 Heisenberg, 'The Decision to Study Physics', in *Physics and Philosophy*, p. 172.

18 Einstein, p. 12.

19 Heisenberg, 'Science and Religion', in *Physics and Philosophy*, p. 11.

20 Krishna Dutta and Andrew Robinson, *Rabindranath Tagore: The Myriad-Minded Man*, London: Bloomsbury Publishing Limited, 1995, p. 14.

21 Rabindranath Tagore, 'Message of Farewell to Canada', delivered to the Fourth Triennial Conference of the National Council of Education of Canada, Vancouver, 14 April, 1929; reprinted in P.C. Mahalanobis, *Rabindranath Tagore's Visit to Canada*, Brooklyn, NY: Haskell House Publishers Ltd., 1977, p. 66.

22 Author unknown, 'A Poet of the Lotus -Sadhana – The Crescent Moon', *The Saturday Review*, 27 December, 1913; reprinted in Sahitya Samsad, *Imagining Tagore: Rabindranath and the British Press (1912–1941)*, Calcutta: Shishu Sahitya Samsad Pvt. Ltd., 2000, p. xxii.

23 From 'Sadhana', his philosophical lectures, given at Harvard University and in London, in 1913. Dutta and Robinson, *Rabindranath Tagore: The Myriad-Minded Man*, p. 361.

24 Tagore, 'My Reminiscences' as quoted in Dutta and Robinson, *Rabindranath Tagore: The Myriad-Minded Man*, p. 361.

25 See: Hermann Weyl, 'Introduction', *Space – Time – Matter*, Henry L. Brose, transl., London: Methuen & Co. Ltd., 1922, pp. 1–10.

26 *Faust: eine historie*, manuscript after J.W. von Goethe, produced by: The Task Force of the Institute for Theoretical Physics, Copenhagen; reprinted in George Gamov, *Thirty Years that Shook Physics: The Story of Quantum Theory*, New York: Dover Publications, Inc., 1966, p. 187.

Defining the North
Searching for a Visual Language

Katerina Atanassova

Fig. 24
**J.E.H. MacDonald
at the Toronto
Arts and Letters
Club**
February, 1913,
Archives of Ontario

Fig. 23
**J.E.H. MacDonald
Cathedral Mountain** (detail)
1927
Oil on paperboard
21.4 x 26.6 cm
McMichael Canadian Art
Collection, Kleinburg,
Ontario, gift of Mr R.A. Laidlaw
(1966.15.8)

Art requires associated ideas in the observer for its appreciation. He must have experiences generally similar to the artist to respond to the art. You will remember the story of the lady talking to Turner about his picture. 'No, really, Mr. Turner, I never saw anything like that in nature', and Turner's reply, 'Very likely not, madam, but don't you wish you had?'[1]

With these words J.E.H. MacDonald began his lecture at the Art Gallery of Toronto on 17 April, 1931. By then a celebrated member of the Group of Seven and a respected art educator, he was reflecting on the time, eighteen years earlier, when he and Lawren Harris travelled to the Albright Art Gallery in Buffalo, New York. They went to see an exhibition of Scandinavian art, then on tour in the United States. The lecture was an insightful overview of the artistic traditions of Norway, Denmark, and Sweden and demonstrated his interest in their nationalistic art. By providing a context for one of the most significant modernist art exhibitions of that era, however, MacDonald was indirectly referring to the public opposition or indifference the artists in the Group of Seven had experienced early on.

By 1931 Tom Thomson and the Group of Seven were celebrated as pioneers who had introduced the Canadian wilderness as a valid artistic subject and linked the 'rugged' northern landscape with modernism. In the thirteen years of their formal existence, the Group held eight exhibitions. In that time they moved steadily from harsh criticism for their modernist approach to wide public acclaim for their portrayal of new territories all across Canada.

Man versus Landscape[2]

Although these artists did not formalise their association until 1920, when they had their first exhibition at the Art Gallery of Toronto, the 1910s were their formative years individually and as a group. They went on sketching trips and painted together, all the while talking about art and pooling their experience. The idea for the Group had its genesis in 1911, a few years after Harris returned from his art studies in Germany, when he visited an exhibition of MacDonald's paintings at the Arts and Letters Club in Toronto.[3] According to him, these were the first paintings he had seen that captured the authentic character of the Canadian countryside. After visiting the Buffalo exhibition, these two artists were inspired by this same basic quality in the Scandinavian landscapes, and they determined to form a nationalist art group to paint the 'real spirit' of Canada directly from unspoiled nature. Harris, a consummate artist and thinker bursting with creative ideas and drive, soon became the leader of the informal group. 'This was a search for a native way of seeing and painting', he wrote years later, 'which could be achieved only if the creative search was animated by the informing spirit of the country itself'.[4]

Tom Thomson was the first to answer the call of the wild. In 1912 he made an extended sketching trip to Algonquin Park, a provincial reserve about three hundred kilometres north of Toronto, and returned with a number of bold and inspiring sketches. They were unlike anything painted by a Canadian artist before, imbued with the character and the spirit of the North. Fellow artists and a few art patrons immediately recognised Thomson's ability to capture his

Fig. 25
Frank Johnston
April, 1913
Archives of Ontario

Fig. 26
**Lawren Harris
at his studio**
25 April, 1926
Archives of Ontario

intuitive bond with nature in all its variety and moods. Algonquin Park and the area around Georgian Bay and Go Home Bay, where Harris's friend Dr James MacCallum had a cottage, became favourite sketching grounds for Thomson and the future members of the Group.[5]

'The first night spent in the North and the thrilling days after were turning points in my life', Lismer wrote to his wife during a trip with Thomson in May 1914. The thrill of these Algonquin trips quickly came to an end, however, with the outbreak of World War One. Jackson enlisted in the army, then Harris. Early in 1918 the Canadian War Records Office appointed Varley as an official war artist. He was joined by Jackson, who had been wounded at the front and transferred to the art department, and they followed the advancing Canadian troops in Western Europe. Together they produced some of the finest paintings for the Canadian War Memorials Fund.

The war had a profound impact on Canadian society—and on the artists who had experienced or documented it. Varley and Jackson returned home in 1919 determined to find a way to express their feelings, not only as Canadians but also as citizens of the larger world. These artist friends increasingly left the city and the confinement of their studios and ventured farther afield, first into the unpopulated Ontario wilderness, then into the west and the north, to discover Canada in its primal glory. 'From the very first, before the Group had a name', Harris wrote, 'our adventure toward painting Canadian themes in a Canadian way had commenced'.[6]

Tracking along the virgin lakes, dense forests, and mountain peaks, they saw themselves as trailblazers and believed that 'some day … the land will return the compliments and believe in the artists'.[7] They wanted to push through the old perceptions and open new frontiers of knowledge. Their romance with the wilderness is obvious in their powerful on-site sketches, which could evoke the very scent of resin in the forest.

In autumn, 1918, MacDonald, Harris, and Johnston joined Dr MacCallum on a sketching trip into Algoma, a rugged forested region of

mountains, canyons, rivers, and waterfalls. They reached this virtually unpopulated terrain via the Algoma Central Railway and lodged in a fitted-out caboose, or boxcar, parked on railway sidings. During the day they travelled by canoe through the water-ways. When they wanted to move on to another painting place, they flagged down a passing train and hitched the boxcar on at the end (see fig. 14, p. 22). This adventurous trip awakened their senses and inspired them—and in the spring of 1919 Harris, MacDonald, and Johnston repeated it along with Jackson. Indeed, the majority of the works shown in the first two exhibitions of the Group of Seven resulted from these sketching trips. The time spent together in the Algoma region helped define a new visual language. This was especially so for Johnston and MacDonald who produced some of their most powerful compositions based on these excursions. Many of the Group's early paintings were suffused with the spirit of adventure and mystery. Lismer's *A September Gale, Georgian Bay* (1921) (sketch, cat. 49), described as 'bold to the point of crudity',[8] epitomized the Group's beliefs. Painted at the same location at Go Home Bay, Varley's *Stormy Weather, Georgian Bay* (1921) (cat. 52) reveals nature's grandeur and unpredictability in a more sensitive and fluid interpretation. Viewed as 'a gesture of symbolic solidarity' with his friends, this painting was the only large landscape Varley produced before he moved west.[9]

Usually peaceful and serene, the land in these two works becomes a vortex, breeding storms with gusty winds and furious rain. The artist must join with it, Varley said, 'emptying ourselves of everything except that Nature is here in all its greatness'.[10] Many contemporary critics declared this new movement 'art gone mad',[11] particularly in the painters' bold use of colour, lack of attention to detail, and vigorous sweeping brushstrokes. Indeed, it would be several years before most Canadians applauded the Group for the beauty they found in the wild – for capturing in paint the nation's soul. All members of the Group were attuned to the sense of the sublime in nature, its vastness and grandeur. They experimented with different techniques, the interplay of forms,

Fig. 27
**Frederick
Horsman Varley**
1929
National Gallery
of Canada Archives

Fig. 28
Franklin Carmichael
1930
National Gallery
of Canada Archives

textures, and the effects of light, and they changed their palettes with the seasons. MacDonald applied these same principles while painting a scene in his own yard, a close-up composition of lush vegetation entitled *The Tangled Garden* (1916). One critic, borrowing a phrase from John Ruskin, accused the artist of throwing 'his pots in the face of the public', but MacDonald included the work in the first group exhibition.[12]

'The results of our exhibitions on the public, the critics and some conservative artists [were] at first a surprise to us', Harris wrote. 'We were called "the hot mush school," and "disordered temperaments"'.[13] Other critical observations focused on the artists' choice of subject matter – primarily landscapes, with little interest in the human figure. But this choice, Lismer explained, was characteristic of the cultural tendencies in Canadian art at the time: 'Landscape painting is the typical expression of new movements in new lands [because] ... the artist is, intuitively, the medium through which this knowledge (so essential to growth) of [the] environment must flow into consciousness ... Today ... wilderness is understood as a source of power'.[14] In *Revelation of Art in Canada*, published in 1926, Harris proclaimed that 'any change of outlook, increase of vision and deepening of conviction in a people shows itself first through some form of art'.[15] Subsequently, he would come to reject the notion that art is based on art itself, and in the 1928–29 *Yearbook of the Arts in Canada* declared that 'our art is founded on a long and growing love and understanding of the North in an ever clearer experience of oneness with the informing spirit of the whole land'.[16]

Varley was the exception: from the start he wanted to paint the human figure in the landscape. His skills as a portrait painter were now recognised, and he received several private commissions. In the first Group exhibition, he entered four portraits, including a study of Barker Fairley.[17] Harris also entered four portraits—a significant number given that he painted only a few in his entire career.

In the catalogue for their second exhibition, in 1921, the Group stated their artistic credo: 'The pictures must speak for themselves'.[18] Carmichael's *October Gold* (1922) (cat. 58), for example, which

was featured at the third exhibition, in 1922, is a true symphony of colour, capturing the Group's desire to seek beauty and grandeur in nature. Their brief forewords pinpoint their interest in experimenting with different goals and techniques. 'Artistic expression is a spirit, not a method', they wrote, 'a pursuit, not a settled goal, an instinct, not a body of rules'.[19]

The artists delayed their next exhibition until January 1925. They were busy making a living or travelling across Canada in search of new painting grounds. By then Lismer had returned to Toronto to join MacDonald at the Ontario College of Art in a full-time teaching position. MacDonald also continued to work as a freelance designer and was actively involved with Toronto's art community. Then the Canadian contribution to the Palace of Arts in Wembley, England, in 1924 marked a turning point for public acceptance of the Group. Well-respected British journalists, including Paul Konody and C. Lewis Hind, showered them with praise. 'These Canadians', wrote Hind, 'are standing on their own feet, revealing their own country with gay virility'.[20] Two years later, at the *Exhibition of Canadian Painting* in New York and, in 1927, at the *Exposition d'art canadien* at the Jeu de Paume in Paris, the Group once again attracted public attention and critical praise.

The artists found that the experience of painting outdoors led them to see landscape as a realm of divine presence – a view supported by the literature, philosophy, and religious attitudes of the time. While searching for the roots of the complexity of the Group's art scholars have traced sources of some of their ideas to the writings of Walt Whitman, Henry David Thoreau and Ralph Waldo Emerson. In *Leaves of Grass* for example, Whitman demonstrates the connection between divinity and roughness, a concept essential to the development of landscape painting in Canada at the time. 'Nature is rude and incomprehensible at first', Whitman declares, 'Be not discouraged – keep on – there are divine things, well envelop'd'.[21] Lawren Harris took this mystical vision a step further when he became interested in the theosophical movement and soon joined the Toronto chapter. MacDonald, a sensitive and

Fig. 29
Arthur Lismer
1930
National Gallery
of Canada Archives

Fig. 30
**A.Y. Jackson in
his studio, Toronto**
1929
National Gallery
of Canada Archives

poetic soul, was also attracted to the writings of Whitman and Thoreau and their ideas helped sharpen his sensitivity to nature. From the 1920s on, in his depictions of mountains or even single trees, Harris combined their geometric forms with spiritual ideas. 'There is an interplay of something we see outside of us with our inner response', he explained. In his essay 'Art Is the Distillate of Life', he justified his reasons for simplifying earthly forms to their essence—what he called the presence of the informing spirit. After 1923, through regular trips to painting locations along the north shores of Lake Superior, he reinforced this tendency in his art.

At this time, Lismer and Varley were struggling to make a living to support their families. Lismer's only time for painting was during family trips to Georgian Bay over the summer, when he was not teaching. Carmichael also had little time for sketching trips, except around Toronto. In the autumn of 1924 he visited the La Cloche region on the north shore of Lake Huron, and it became his favourite painting location. He built his summer home there, and the open vista overlooking the rolling hills provided inspiration for many of his works.

Defining the North: Searching for a Visual Language

Lake Superior is the largest and deepest of the Great Lakes and the world's biggest inland sea.[22] Harris and Jackson first visited its north shore after a sketching trip in Algoma in 1921. Fascinated by the area, particularly the contrasts between the menacing black rocks and the silvery shimmer of its waters, they returned numerous times. In his autobiography, *A Painter's Country*, Jackson explained that they went there because Harris found the Algoma country too opulent for his work. He preferred the austerity of this fire-swept and barren northern land.

In communion with nature in this setting, Harris understood the necessity of artistic growth, and he moved from the particulars of his surroundings to the universal in art. There he sought to penetrate nature's inner sanctum. *Pic Island* (c. 1924) (cats. 107–108), inaccessible in its steep slopes, resembles a hostile dark animal looming over a lake. Harris was determined to venture into the unknown. Like Whitman he believed that nature was formed and informed by the spirit, therefore every organic form in his art, every tree or mountain became a symbol of a greater spiritual reality. Concrete shapes refer to specific geographical locations like Pic Island, yet the austerity and the distance created between the viewer and the place – wrapped in unexpected light – make this scene more celestial than earthly.

Harris juxtaposes the sharp contours of the island against the soft background of sky and water. He often used this composition in his work from Lake Superior trips, placing the more tender and poetic side of nature against a powerful presence with chromatic strength. Some critics argue that he captured the Canadian psyche in these works, both in its lyricism and its strict apprehension of reality.[23] Feeling strongly the responsibility of an artist to translate the appearance of natural forms into spiritual terms he wrestled constantly to marry the laws of art with those of nature. In this lay the tension and ambiguity between his aesthetic beliefs and his artistic vision. The fourth Group exhibition in 1925 included fewer works but covered a much larger geographical area. By then only Jackson and Harris were painting full-time and were free to travel extensively, so they contributed more works than the other members. Their paintings of the Canadian Rocky Mountains attracted the most attention. One reviewer found in these works 'that out-pouring vigour, that will and flowing power, [which] is the essence of the Canadian spirit'.[24]

The Mystery of the West

An adventurer by heart, Jackson was the first of the Group to visit the Canadian Rockies, in 1914, inspiring most of his friends to travel out west and discover their timeless beauty and grandeur. MacDonald made his first trip to the Rockies in 1924 and, over the next five years, went to different locations to paint. In the summer of 1924 Harris also had his first taste of the Rockies, at Lake O'Hara.

Varley had his first glimpse of the mountains at Banff, which he visited after completing portrait commissions in Winnipeg and Edmonton in 1924. He was smitten by western Canada, where he was received like a celebrity. 'The artist is a wonderful man to them', he wrote, 'but he belongs altogether to an unknown land'.[25] After his success as a war artist and during his early stay in Ontario Varley kept busy with graphic design work and portrait commissions, yet his friends were becoming increasingly concerned about his welfare. Barker Fairley warned, '[h]is nature cannot serve two masters and if he had to turn again to commercial work for any length of time I believe that he would stop painting'.[26]

To his friends' surprise, Varley accepted a position to teach at the Vancouver School of Decorative and Applied Arts in 1926. Before long he found the natural beauty of British Columbia to be a source of endless artistic inspiration. He sketched on Grouse Mountain in Vancouver and made summer trips to Garibaldi Provincial Park and Black Tusk, often in the company of his students and colleagues. The dark thrusting silhouettes of the mountain peaks, the brilliant translucent colours of the glaciers, and the reflections in the emerald green waters of the mountain lakes and the Pacific Ocean thrilled his imaginative eye. *West Coast Sunset, Vancouver* (1926) demonstrates again Varley's ability to transcend spatial definitions and carry that open-air wind-driven expansiveness of scenery, as in *Stormy Weather, Georgian Bay*. But if the vista was thrilling to his eye, at first the experience was not as inspiring as he expected. 'The weather is wearing'; he wrote to Arthur Lismer, 'incessant rain, mountains blotted out for weeks'.[27] By then his newly awakened sense for the landscape and the human presence in it had turned to new compositional devices. With the application of his spiritual greens throughout, and the open middle-ground of the canvas, Varley succeeds in achieving a moment of serenity and unity with nature.

'Varley gave Vancouver the first genuine tingling sort of big excitement of art', said former student Jack Shadbolt, 'and we were all so proud that he was here and working among us'.[28] Varley continued to contribute to the Group of Seven exhibitions, and, during these western years, he produced his best and most invigorating portraits and landscapes. Lynn Valley was one of Varley's favourite spots—a picturesque, sparsely populated area nestled on the outskirts of North Vancouver. By this time Varley had left his wife and four children and become romantically involved with his student Vera Weatherbie. They often took the trolley from Vancouver to explore this area, and *Lynn Valley* (1932–35) (cat. 98) captures one of its majestic views.

Varley's growing interest in Asian art at the time helped to expand his understanding of the symbolic dimension of landscape. In *The Cloud, Red Mountain* (1928) (cat. 96) the artist's sense of freedom is expressed through his special arrangement of forms in vivid red offset by green. His symbolic use of colour combines the real and the ideal realms while setting them apart. 'It is wonderful', he wrote to a friend describing the exaltation from his mountain trips, 'to leave the sheltered town [of Vancouver] & in two hours time be up in a dazzling white world,

Fig. 31
Frederick Horsman Varley
Dharana
c. 1932
Oil on canvas
86.4 × 101.6 cm
Art Gallery of Ontario, Toronto, gift from the Albert H. Robson Memorial Subscription Fund, 1942

Fig. 32
**Frederick
Horsan Varley
Vera**
c. 1935
Oil on canvas
90.8 x 70.5
The Thomson
Collection,
Art Gallery of
Ontario, Toronto

full of fantastic forms, wind carved & polished, where one can bathe in prismatic colours, incredibly pure.[29] The setting for *Dharana* (1933) (fig. 31), one of Varley's iconic works, was an abandoned fire ranger's hut overlooking the valley. The choice of title referred to the spiritual qualities he came to know in Vera's personality and her incredible ability seemingly to become one with her surroundings.[30] The lovers had climbed the road above the valley and discovered the hut. There they shared many happy hours, painting on the roofed porch and rejoicing in the views before them.

Varley's work during the decade in British Columbia is imbued with the emotional re-awakening brought about by his communion with the surroundings and his passionate love affair with Vera. In *Portrait of Vera* (c. 1935) (fig. 32), the background he chose draws on the Chinese tradition of landscape painting, suggesting free movement and translucent colouring. This background is compositionally connected to the figure through its vertical lines, which resonate with her standing pose. Varley saw Vera as a

spiritual person, a passionate interpreter of nature, and he captured that feeling in her portrait.

Harris also found new harmony for his work in the west. Between 1924 and 1928 he spent his summers in the Rockies, trekking along the Tonquin Valley, Maligne Lake, Lake Louise, Moraine Lake, Lake O'Hara, Emerald Lake, Yoho and Jasper National Parks, and the distant Mount Robson.[31] The Rockies became a metaphor for his spiritual beliefs: the mountains represented the human journey, and the summits the conquests of life's struggle to attain ultimate freedom. At the time Harris painted Mount Lefroy (1930) (cats. 113–116), his theosophical beliefs were central to his search for truth. Some scholars have seen elements of prayer, the link between the earthly and the heavenly spheres, in this serene work. Harris himself considered it of major importance and selected it for the 1932 *Exhibition of Contemporary Canadian Artists* at the Roerich Museum in New York City.

Understanding Harris's philosophy is the key to interpreting his art. The forms and colours he used were just the departure point in the ascent to spiritual enlightenment. This approach can be traced back to medieval iconography — Harris replaces the divine with nature. Harris's *Cathedral Mountain* (1927) (fig. 33) refers to nature as a spiritual edifice. Some critics argue that this work was not based on nature but presented a platonic idea of a mountain or even an infinite mathematical series of mountain impressions.[32] In comparison, MacDonald's *Cathedral Mountain* (cat. xx) captures the physical quality of the scenery, the majesty and sheer beauty of the surroundings.

On Top of the World

The Canadian Arctic, in its glacial breadth and glory, its myriad images and legends, forms one of the foundations of the Canadian soul. Many artists have ventured there to experience their own discovery. In addition to the awe-inspiring scenery, northbound trips in the early twentieth century were a daring adventure for southern travellers. For Jackson, Harris, and Varley, each journey became a kind of spiritual cleansing, a chance to discover a new concept of life that made a deep and lasting impression. Jackson was the first of the Group to go there, in the summer of 1927. He joined his friend Dr Frederick Banting, the co-discoverer of insulin, on the steamer *Beothic* as it made its regular supply visits to northern outposts.

In 1930 Harris joined Jackson and sailed within a few hundred kilometres of the North Pole (see fig. 19, p. 26). This long and challenging journey provided yet another stimulus for Harris's unceasing artistic and spiritual quest, and his next series of paintings featured the towering exuberant shapes of icebergs floating in frigid seas.

When Harris and Jackson included paintings from their Arctic trips in an exhibition at the Art Gallery of Toronto in 1930, they stirred great interest among the art community.[33] Their interpretation of the North – the home of the Inuit – conveyed the close bond between these northern people and the inhospitable territory they inhabit, an expanse of ice and snow stretching to the horizon. The Arctic landscape is a unique subject for an artist. It presents a remarkable contrast between the land, which remains fixed and therefore constant, and the ever-changing atmospheric conditions. On closer observation, the visiting members from the Group found other more subtle signs of change that threatened the traditional way of life of the indigenous population and their culture. Banting and Jackson, scientist and artist, united in their attempts to warn Canadians of these threats. When Varley travelled north in 1938, his art reflected this same sentiment.

Like Jackson and Harris, Varley felt that his northern sojourn signalled a true revelation. The excitement he felt during his nearly three-month journey on board the supply ship *Nascopie* made him 'drunk with the seemingly impossible'. He wanted to paint the stillness of the North and the exact gradations of radiant light, shifting at any time of day or night. 'On dreary days colour became more precious', Varley told a radio host on his return. 'Ice-floes splinter light into colour, and green of all greens, the translucent glacial green of ice beneath the water, the pure violet light edging hollow caves'.[34] For both Varley and Harris, the trip to the Arctic left an indelible impression on their psyches and satisfied their thirst for the sublime.

Keeping Pace with the Innovations of the 1930s

The foreword to the exhibition catalogue in 1931 proclaimed: 'The physical trails run north, east and west – but mostly north – into the heart of the country, away from the cities. The most significant trail has been cut into the spiritual and national life of the country, challenging apathy, and giving a new rhythm to the forward stride of a people'.[35]

The position of the founding members of the Group of Seven had changed dramatically since the early 1920s. From pioneers as modernist artists, they had become leaders of a national art movement and had received both acclaim and criticism. Some opponents were already suggesting that their work had become formulaic.

Fig. 33
Lawren Harris
Cathedral Mountain, Morning Light
1926
Oil on board
30.5 x 38 cm
Private collection

After the 1930 exhibition, Bertram Brooker, the first Canadian abstract artist, put it this way: 'The present show at Toronto rings the death knell of the Group of Seven as a unified and dominant influence in Canadian painting ... The experimentation is over, the old aggressiveness has declined'.[36]

Over the years, three new artists joined the Group of Seven: A.J. Casson, Edwin Holgate, and L.L. FitzGerald. After 1925 membership became more flexible, and different artists were invited to exhibit as guests with the Group. Harris's reputation as a mentor was vital for the younger generation who were trying to follow in their footsteps. After meeting in 1927 with Emily Carr, accepted today as one of Canada's best-known female painters, Harris gave strong support to other women artists and welcomed them as guests in the Group's subsequent exhibitions.

In 1927 Harris played a key role in bringing the International Exhibition of Modern Art, organized by the Société Anonyme, to the Art Gallery of Toronto – the most important international art exhibition shown in Canada to that date. Established around the same time as the Group, the Société Anonyme was a vital force in introducing modern art to American audiences and providing a forum for contemporary artists.

By the early 1930s the Group of Seven had served its purpose. In his autobiography, Jackson attributes the dissolution of the Group to MacDonald's sudden death in 1932 and the departure of Harris and Lismer from Toronto.[37]

Harris left in 1934 and moved to Hanover, New Hampshire, where, for the next few years, his artistic output decreased. *Winter Comes from the Arctic to the Temperate Zone* (c. 1935) is one of the few transitional works he painted during this period (fig. 34). Although it portrays organic forms, Harris was already experimenting with abstraction, and this composition manifests his belief in life as a spiritual energy.

The founding members were growing apart and now enjoyed success as artists on their own. They no longer needed to exhibit together to confront hostile reviewers and attract art collectors to buy their paintings. A few of them contributed to an exhibition in 1933. It included twenty-six new artists and led seamlessly to the formation of a new group of artists, the Canadian Group of Painters, with Harris and Jackson as founding members.

The Legacy

What makes Group of Seven images so appealing to today's Canadian audiences? Is it the romantic view of remote geographical locations that are no longer the same? Or the spiritual powers of nature, with her stillness and quiet? Whatever it is, the Canadian wilderness remains a distant yet familiar spiritual journey for generations of Canadians.

The Group's single most important achievement was that, through their art, these men introduced Canadians to new frontiers of knowledge – to the savage beauty of the landscape throughout the country. Their clarity of vision and simplicity of theme and treatment inspired other Canadian artists to produce art that was profoundly national in feeling, but universal in its breadth. This tenacious desire to remain true to their identity is their lasting contribution to Canadian painting.

MacDonald's lecture in 1931 contained a prophetic wish for the acceptance of Canadian art abroad. 'A Canadian exhibition in the Scandinavian countries might now prove almost as interesting and inspiring to them as their art was to us at Buffalo', he said. 'I am sure they would realize an affinity of inspiration, which is probably the unifying element in all art appreciation'.[38] That affinity is everything viewers need to appreciate the art of Tom Thomson and the Group of Seven.

Fig. 34
Lawren Harris
Winter Comes from the Arctic to the Temperate Zone
c. 1935
Oil on canvas
74.1 x 91.2 cm
McMichael Canadian Art Collection, Kleinburg, Canada, purchase 1994 (1994.13)

Notes

1 J.E.H. MacDonald, 'Scandinavian Art' (lecture, Art Gallery of Toronto [now Art Gallery of Ontario], April 17, 1931; reprinted in *Northward Journal*, nos. 18/19 [1980]: p. 9). The original lecture is in the artist's archive at Library and Archives Canada, Ottawa (LAC).

2 'Man versus Landscape' is a reference to an article Barker Fairley published in December 1939 in the magazine *Canadian Forum* on the development of Canadian painting. Fairley, a professor at the University of Toronto, was a strong supporter of the Group of Seven and often joined them at the Arts and Letters Club.

3 Lawren Harris, 'The Story of the Group of Seven', in *Group of Seven*, exh. cat., Vancouver: Vancouver Art Gallery, 1954, p. 9.

4 Harris, 'The Story of the Group of Seven', p. 9.

5 Thanks to support from Dr MacCallum, who shared the vision for a nationalistic art movement, Thomson was able to resign from his job as a commercial designer at the Grip Ltd. in 1914 and devote himself that year to painting.

6 Lawren Harris, 'The Story of the Group of Seven', p. 9.

7 Art Gallery of Toronto, foreword to *Exhibition of Paintings by the Group of Seven*, 1921.

8 Madge Macbeth, 'The All Canadian Exhibition of Paintings at Ottawa', *Saturday Night*, 41, no. 17 (13 March, 1926), p. 25.

9 Christopher Varley, *F.H. Varley: A Centennial Exhibition*, Edmonton: Edmonton Art Gallery, 1981, p. 58.

10 Sheffield City Archives, Varley Papers. F.H. Varley to Ethel Varley (copy), n.d. (May 1914).

11 Quoted in Charles C. Hill, *The Group of Seven: Art for a Nation*, Toronto: McClelland & Stewart, 1995.

12 Hector Charlesworth, 'Pictures That Can Be Heard: A Survey of the Ontario Society Exhibition', *Saturday Night*, 29, no. 23 (18 March, 1916), pp. 5, 11.

13 Lawren Harris, 'The Story of the Group of Seven', p. 11.

14 Arthur Lismer, 'Art in Canada', *The Twentieth Century*, 2, no. 1 (November 1933).

15 Lawren Harris, 'Revelation of Art in Canada', *Canadian Theosophist*, 7/5 (1926), p. 85.

16 Lawren Harris, 'Creative Art and Canada', in Bertram Brooker, ed., *The Yearbook of the Arts in Canada*, Toronto: Macmillan, 1929, p. 185.

17 Two other portraits, one of J.E.H. MacDonald and one of Winifred Head, are lost. For a more detailed survey of Varley's portraits, see Katerina Atanassova, *F.H. Varley: Portraits into the Light*, Toronto: Dundurn Press, 2006.

18 Art Gallery of Toronto, foreword to *Exhibition of Paintings by the Group of Seven*, 1921.

19 Art Gallery of Toronto, *Group of Seven Exhibition of Paintings*, 1922.

20 C. Lewis Hind, 'Life and I', *Daily Chronicle*, 30 April, 1924.

21 Walt Whitman, *Leaves of Grass*, New York: Grosset and Dunlap, 1971, p. 111.

22 Barbara Chisholm and Andrea Gutsche, *Superior: Under The Shadow of The Gods*, Toronto: Lynx Images Inc., 1998, p. XIII.

23 Ann Davis, *The Logic of Ecstasy, Canadian Mystical Painting 1920–1940*, Toronto: University of Toronto Press Inc., 1992, p. 62.

24 Bess Housser, 'In the Realm of Art: Impressions of the Group of Seven', *The Canadian Bookman*, 7, no. 2 (February 1925), p. 33.

25 F.H. Varley to Maud Varley, 2 April, 1924, Varley Papers, MG 30 D401, LAC.

26 Barker Fairley to Eric Brown, director of the National Gallery of Canada, 4 December, 1921, National Gallery of Canada Archives, Ottawa.

27 Peter Varley, *Frederick H. Varley,* Toronto: Key Porter Books, 1983, p. 110.

28 Jack Shadbolt, quoted in Maria Tippett, *Stormy Weather, F.H. Varley, A Biography*, Toronto: McClelland & Stewart, 1998, p. 159.

29 McMichael Canadian Art Collection, Varley Papers, Varley to Arnold (?), 15 April, 1929.

30 The works of Augustus John and Dante Gabriel Rossetti have been pointed out as a possible influence for the title as well. In her biography of Varley, Maria Tippett points out that John's *Hark, Hark the Lark* was exhibited in 1903 at the Carfax Gallery in London, while Rossetti's *Beata Beatrix* was by then in the collection of the Tate Gallery in London.

31 Lisa Christensen, *A Hiker's Guide to the Rocky Mountain Art of Lawren Harris*, Calgary: Fifth House Publishing, 2000, pp. 42–72.

32 Hill, *Art for a Nation*, p. 10.

33 Hill, *The Group of Seven*, p. 261.

34 Art Gallery of Ontario, Varley Papers, F.H. Varley, '"Nascoie", CBC Radio Talk', 1938, p. 2.

35 Art Gallery of Toronto, *Catalogue of an Exhibition of the Group of Seven*, 1930.

36 Bertram Brooker, 'The Seven Arts', *Ottawa Citizen*, 19 April, 1930. Quoted in Charles Hill, *Canadian Painting in the Thirties*, exh. cat., Ottawa: National Gallery of Canada, 1975, p. 21.

37 A.Y. Jackson, *A Painter's Country: The Autobiography of A.Y. Jackson*, Toronto: Clarke Irwin, 1958, p. 118.

38 MacDonald, 'Scandinavian Art', p. 10.

'This is what we want to do with Canada'[1] Reflections of Scandinavian Landscape Painting in the Work of Tom Thomson and the Group of Seven

Nils Ohlsen

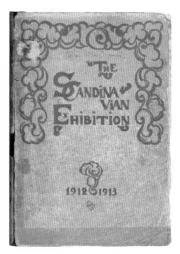

Fig. 36
Exhibition of Contemporary Scandinavian Art
1913
Buffalo: Albright Art Gallery,
McMichael Canadian Art
Collection Library, gift of
Thoreau MacDonald

Fig. 35
Lawren Harris
Winter (detail)
1914, oil on panel
25.9 x 33.1 cm
Collection: A.K. Prakash
Exhibited only in London and Oslo

You instinctively feel, on studying these canvases, an exhilarating sense of direct communication with nature and natural forces. You note the naïve zest of healthy, unfatigued sensibilities for fresh, tonic colour contrasts, and you feel the thrill of eternal aspiration in this fondness for great, open spaces and the magic radiance of the arctic aurora.[2]

This quotation describes perfectly the landscape painting of Tom Thomson and the Group of Seven, but in fact it comes from the catalogue of the 'Exhibition of Contemporary Scandinavian Art' mounted by the American Scandinavian Society in New York. No fewer than three kings acted as patrons of this show when it opened on 10 December 1912 in the American Art Galleries: their majesties Gustav V of Sweden, Christian X of Denmark and Haakon VII of Norway. As a representative of the art world, the curator responsible for the exhibition could certainly hold his own in this illustrious company: Christian Brinton was an internationally respected American critic and exhibition organiser whose interests went far beyond the familiar Western schools. Moreover, the museum directors and art

historians who acted as his co-curators were people who set the tone in the visual arts in the three participating Scandinavian countries, Denmark, Sweden and Norway.[3] By the standards of the day the accompanying catalogue was a lavish affair, with over 170 pages, biographies of all the artists and a large number of reproductions of paintings. It featured 165 works by forty-five of the most prominent Scandinavian artists practising at the turn of the twentieth century. Over the following months the exhibition toured to Buffalo (Albright Art Gallery), Toledo (Museum of Arts), Chicago (Art Institute of Chicago) and Boston (Museum of Fine Arts).

The timing and the ambitious nature of the exhibition were no accident. There existed a long-standing enthusiasm for the North, but in December 1911 the Norwegian Roald Amundsen had discovered the South Pole and this triggered a renewed surge of interest. Humanists and romantics had already been fascinated by the Nordic myths and sagas,[4] but in the *fin de siècle* period a fully fledged craze developed for the romance of the North, prompted not least by the discovery of Scandinavia as a travel destination and stoked by the most prominent of all *Nordlandfahrer* (Nordic travellers), the German emperor Wilhelm II. The North figured in the imagination as a paradisical place of refuge for Central Europeans wearied and disillusioned by the modern world.[5] Once deemed the mystical home of savage and primitive peoples, shrouded in gloom, it now shone out as a model country, pointing the way forwards. Norway and Finland, sparsely populated countries that had fought long for their independence and were young in historical terms, provided particularly welcome blank canvases on which to project modern ideas about society.[6] The visual arts and the work of the writers Henrik Ibsen, Bjørnstjerne Bjørnson and August Strindberg, whose plays and novels enjoyed great international success, contributed immensely to this image.

The official goal of the exhibition was 'to show American Scandinavians, in the most favourable and acceptable manner, the production of the leading Swedish, Danish and Norwegian painters'.[7] Today it is known to have far exceeded this aim. For two Canadians visiting the exhibition in Buffalo, it proved a crucial experience with far-reaching consequences. Neither J.E.H. MacDonald nor his fellow artist Lawren Harris, twelve years his junior, had ever been to a Scandinavian country or engaged with Scandinavian art. In Buffalo they encountered works of art that did much more than awaken their interest and excite their praise.

For the two Canadians seeking to plumb 'the character, the power and clarity and rugged elemental beauty of our own land'[8] Scandinavian art will have come less as a surprise than as

an encouragement. MacDonald and Harris immediately sensed a deep spiritual affinity when faced with the Scandinavian works. 'Harris was deeply impressed by the sympathies it awoke in him. In subject, in treatment, there was a pronounced affinity with his own aspirations and with the aim of his colleagues'.[9] 'Here were a large number of paintings which gave body to our rather nebulous ideas', Harris recalled in 1949.[10] 'Here was an art, bold, vigorous and uncompromising, embodying direct experience of the great North'.[11] In a similar vein to Harris, MacDonald later wrote of the exhibition:

We were full of associated ideas. Not that we had ever been to Scandinavia, but we had feelings of height and breadth and depth and colour and sunshine and solemnity and new wonder about our own country, and we were pretty pleased to find a correspondence with these feelings of ours, not only in the general attitude of the Scandinavian artists, but also in the natural aspects of their countries. Except in minor points, the pictures might all have been Canadian and we felt, 'This is what we want to do with Canada' … These artists seemed to be a lot of men not trying to express themselves so much as trying to express something that took hold of themselves. The painters began with nature rather than art.[12]

Clearly, the two Canadians could not contain their enthusiasm. Sudden revelation and *déjà vu* must have coincided. A huge door swung open, offering them a view of how they might realise their own aims. What had previously been a vague quest, now

Fig. 37
Jens Ferdinand Willumsen
Jotunheim
1892–93
Oil on canvas, wood, painted zinc and enamel on copper
150 × 270 cm
The J.F. Willumsen Museum, Frederikssund, Denmark

Fig. 38
Gustav Fjæstad
Vintermånsken (Winter Moonlight)
1895
Oil on canvas
100 x 134 cm
Nationalmuseum
Stockholm

Fig. 39
Harald Sohlberg
Vinternatt i fjellene (Winter Night in the Mountains)
1901
Oil on canvas
70 x 92 cm
Private collection

Fig. 40
Prins Eugen
Den ljusa natten, Tyresö (The Bright Night, Tyresö)
1899
Oil on canvas
40 x 100 cm
Prins Eugens
Waldemarsudde,
Stockholm

acquired a firm footing and a precise direction.

In 1913, Harris and MacDonald were not alone in seeking to formulate a nationally-centred art. Their artist friends Tom Thomson, Franklin Carmichael, A.Y. Jackson, Frank Johnston, Arthur Lismer and Frederick Varley had likewise been engaged since 1910 in a search for a modern and truly Canadian landscape art, going on painting expeditions – often together – in the wilds of Ontario and in the province's Muskoka district and Georgian Bay. Even if only two members of what was still an unnamed association of artists saw the Scandinavian exhibition in Buffalo, a spark was ignited there that led to one of Canada's finest artistic achievements in the twentieth century: the art of Tom Thomson and the Group of Seven.

Comparison of the Scandinavian paintings exhibited in Buffalo with subsequent works by the Canadians quickly reveals the 'correspondence' alluded to by MacDonald. Notes written by MacDonald in his copy of the catalogue confirm that the landscapes left the deepest impression.[13] Special mention should be made in this connection of the Swedes Gustav Fjaestad (fig. 38), Prince Eugen (fig. 40) and Otto Hesselbom, the Norwegians Harald Sohlberg (fig. 39), Thorlof Holmboe, Arne Kavli and Edvard Munch, and the Dane J.F. Willumsen (fig. 37).[14] No Finns took part in the exhibition – Finland does not belong to Scandinavia – but one Finnish artist must be cited since the Canadians' landscapes resemble his just as closely as those of the Scandinavians named above. This is Akseli Gallen-Kallela, whose work was exhibited in the States in 1915–16 and in 1923–24.[15]

Many of the Scandinavian works showed panoramic views of natural landscapes with unspoilt forests, lakes, fjords and mountains, devoid of human life. They were essentially naturalistic and 'correct' in terms of perspective, yet they also evinced varying degrees and styles of abstraction. While Sohlberg cultivated realistic detail to an almost surreal extent, Munch dissolved his landscapes in painterly atmosphere. Willumsen tended to accommodate his subjects to a mosaic-like overall structure with strong colour contrasts, whereas Fjaestad's close-up views of forests reveal a pervasive composition of filigree ornament.

Finally, Jonas Helmer Osslund and Hesselbom simplified detail in order to construct their panoramic views from larger organic forms. All these painters led the viewer from a narrow platform area in the foreground, via a relatively undifferentiated middle ground to a mountain or other striking feature in the distance, creating 'unfathomable and magnificent emotional landscape spaces'[16] that generated an effect of sublime monumentality. It was the 'simplicity of subject matter and presentation' that made a lasting impression on MacDonald.[17] Brinton evoked the same kind of response when he wrote in the catalogue: 'There is one fact which stands clearly forth after a comprehensive survey of Scandinavian painting and it is that … the primal, elementary basis of this art has remained unchanged. It continues, as always, full of tender lyricism and heroic intensity'.[18]

Scandinavian painting of the two decades after 1890 is now generally referred to as *Stimmungsmalerei* (mood painting), in which the painted landscape represents the landscape of the soul. Such idealised images, conceived and constructed around a certain mood, typically feature transitions from day to night for example, or from autumn to winter or sunlight to stormy weather. Nature appears as the locus of an emotional experience, inviting empathetic immersion in a mood more than physical exploration in the mind's eye. Reflections, for instance, can function as echoes of psychological states, distant mountain ranges as focuses of longing. These thematic, compositional and atmospheric aspects of Scandinavian landscape painting recur in the work of Thomson and the Group of Seven.

Yet there are also differences. In explaining these, it should be noted that Canada's entry into the First World War in August 1914 had a severely disruptive effect on these pioneering Canadian artists. Thomson died tragically in Canada in 1917, and not until 1919 did the others start functioning again as a group. An appreciable gap in time therefore separated their art from that of the Scandinavians, and this is naturally reflected in the style of their painting, particularly in its greater degree of abstraction. This is especially noticeable in the

handling. The Canadians substituted a summary treatment of form, rendered by means of impasto patches, monochrome areas and stripes (see fig. 41), for the Scandinavians' realistic or more traditionally painterly approach. In addition, the Canadian paintings evince a slightly different approach to nature. While the Scandinavians occasionally included signs of human settlement and cultivation of the landscape, the Canadians restricted human presence in their pictures to tents, canoes and small huts. In both cases, nature is the leading player in a spectacle as magnificent as it is unapproachable, but the Canadian paintings are more dramatic and richer in contrasts. Whereas the Scandinavians bathe their landscapes in a soft, diffused light, the Canadians favour harsh light that casts bold shadows. They replace the Scandinavians' propensity towards peace and harmony with a penchant for powerful chromatic contrasts in images featuring violent flooding, forest fires, brewing storms and monumental cloud formations. Their compositions therefore tend to be conceived more openly than the essentially closed structures of the Scandinavians'. If the latter can be said to evoke yearning for things past, then the Canadians' paintings conjure up forces of nature that herald change.

In an essay on Scandinavian and American landscape painting in the second half of the nineteenth century Barbara Novak speaks of 'A Shared "Look"… tempered to a large extent by its distance from the European painterly mainstream, and also by the existence of a strong parallel indigenous folk tradition'.[19] This mixture proved highly potent in the development not only of the art of the Canadians, but also in that of other North American artists, such as Marsden Hartley (1877–1943), Arthur Dove (1880–1946) and August Vincent Tack (1870–1949).[20]

Despite the differences between them, Scandinavian and Canadian landscape paintings encapsulate a common view of nature as magnificent, sublime and infinite. Profoundly moved by the grandeur and vastness of their native lands, the artists transformed their impressions into symphonic spatial panoramas that instinctively arouse sublime, even religious, feelings in the viewer. Lawren Harris and Fjaestad engaged intensively with

Fig. 41
J.E.H. MacDonald
Sketch for Beaver
Dam (detail)
1919
Oil on board
21.2 x 26.7 cm
Collection of the
Faculty Club,
University of Toronto

Fig. 42
Johann
Christian Dahl
Vinter ved
Sognefjorden
(Winter at
Sognefjord)
1827
Oil on canvas
61.5 x 75.5 cm
The National
Museum of Art,
Architecture and
Design, Oslo

theosophy.[21] Yet it is not only in their work that the splendour and immensity of nature conveys awareness or intimations of the divine in general and a quest for a shared essence of religious truth in particular. Comparing Scandinavian and American landscape art in the mid nineteenth century, Barbara Novak points out that the similarities between them resulted from a process involving complex cultural factors and notes that the 'idea of self in relation to nature and God or nature as God is… closely allied to this'.[22] Torsten Gunnarsson writes: 'Both the Americans and the Scandinavians had access to the ideas of Schelling and the German idealist philosophers, to Rousseau's natural primitivism, to all the international currents that found God in nature',[23] adding: 'The Conception of Nature as a spiritual entity and a symbol of God's existence became just as widely current [in North America] as in European Romanticism. In America, though, this view of nature conflicted more overtly than in Europe'.[24] This religious element, which sometimes makes the panoramic landscapes seem like modern devotional images, is implicit in the works of both the Scandinavians and the Canadians.

Topographical similarities between Scandinavia and Canada, with their huge areas of unspoiled terrain, formed the basis of this artistic affinity. In related, compelling ways the painters addressed issues of national identity and pantheism against a background of rapid development and cultivation of hitherto untamed natural surroundings previously perceived as threatening.

The art historical foundations of this parallel development lay in a shared Romantic tradition. For example, both groups of artists had frequent recourse to the motif of a foreground tree standing before a wide expanse of landscape, a motif more strongly rooted in the tradition of Scandinavian painting than in any other. Johan Christian Dahl, the founder of independent Norwegian painting in the period after 1814 and a close friend of Caspar David Friedrich in Dresden, used it on several occasions. Heroic and monumental, a single birch tree appears in each case above a deep abyss, defying the forces of nature in front of a wide-ranging mountain landscape. In Dahl's work, as in Thomson's well-known painting *The Jack Pine*, the motif has been interpreted as symbolising a nation's fight for independence. No less revealing is a comparison between Dahl's *Winter at Sognefjord* of 1827 (fig. 42) and Harris's *North Shore, Lake Superior* (see fig. 8, page 16), painted in 1926. Across a gap of almost one hundred years both works convey the sense of the twin characteristics of everlastingness and transitoriness in natural surroundings as forbidding as they are fascinating.

Early nineteenth-century Romantic pictorial concepts and symbolism reached North America at mid-century in the work of the Hudson River School. In his 'Essay on American scenery' of 1835, the school's founder, Thomas Cole, wrote: 'Go not abroad in search of material for the exercise of your pencil, while the virgin charms of our native lands have claims on your deepest affections… Untrammelled as he is, and free from academic and other restraints by virtue of his position, why should not the [American] landscape painter, in accordance with the spirit of self-government, boldly originate a hight [sic] and independent style, based on his native resources?'[25] Coles's wish certainly reached fulfilment in the painting of Thomson and the Group of Seven, even if these artists did make a close study of European, especially Scandinavian, art.

At the Scandinavian Society's exhibition it was probably the art of the Norwegians, a people who had won their battle for independence as recently as 1905, that encouraged the Canadians most emphatically to 'boldly originate a high and independent style'. Jens Thiis, writing about the Norwegian contribution in the catalogue, stated: 'With this newborn faith in actuality, this pantheistic enthusiasm for nature and truth, the men of the eighties wrote, spoke and painted'.[26] And in his introduction Christian Brinton left no doubt as to the fact that he was pinning his hopes on the Norwegians as the source of an independent American art: 'Full of undeveloped power and passionate defiance, more fundamentally talented than the Swedes, and endowed with an aggressive force often disconcerting to the pacific Danes, the Norwegians were able, within the span of a few brief, tempestuous years, to place themselves abreast of their more advantageously situated neighbours'.[27] He introduced these remarks by noting: 'Norway enjoys the distinction of having evolved, during the dim, legendary days of her intrepid Vikings and sea rovers, a thoroughly original and independent national style… Although boasting what should logically have proved a magnificently fruitful legacy, contemporary Norwegian painting owes little or nothing to the past'.[28]

The history of Scandinavian art in the nineteenth and early twentieth centuries is marked by influence from countries outside Scandinavia – with the notable exception of the impact made by the early nineteenth-century Golden Age of Danish art. Scandinavians were drawn to the academies in Dresden, Karlsruhe, Düsseldorf, Munich and, from the 1880s, Paris – and it was there that they acquired their most important experience. Towards the end of the century there was a general move to return home, and only then did Scandinavian artists establish an independent brand of neo-Romantic art. Their role was reversed in relation to Canada: Scandinavians, not least Norwegians, provided the essential impetus behind the foundation of one of Canada's most important groups of artists in the first half of the twentieth century.

That is reason enough to welcome the extensive presentation of work by Tom Thomson and the Group of Seven in 2011–12 not only in London and Groningen, but also in the Nationalgalerie in Oslo. Further cause for celebration is provided by the scheduled recreation in 2012 in New York of the Scandinavian Art Exhibition mounted in the city by the American Scandinavian Society a century earlier. In more than one respect that exhibition caught the mood of the times and made a significant contribution to the history of art.

Notes

1 J.E.H. MacDonald, in Charles C. Hill, *The Group of Seven: Art for a Nation*, exh. cat., National Gallery of Canada, Ottawa, 1995, p. 48.

2 Christian Brinton, 'Introductory note', in *American Scandinavian Society: Exhibition of Contemporary Scandinavian Art*, exh. cat., American Art Galleries, New York, 1912, p. 26.

3 Karl Madsen was director of the Royal Gallery in Copenhagen; the Swede Carl G. Laurin was a writer, art historian and teacher whose home formed a major focus of artistic life in Stockholm; and Jens Thiis was director of the National Gallery in Christiania (now Oslo).

4 Julia Zernack, 'Nordenschwärmerei und Germanenbegeisterung im Kaiserreich', in *Wahlverwandtschaft: Skandinavien und Deutschland 1800 bis 1914*, Berlin, 1997, p. 71.

5 Zernack, 'Nordenschwärmerei und Germanenbegeisterung im Kaiserreich', p. 71.

6 Norway and Finland did not achieve independence until the early twentieth century, whereas Denmark and Sweden had already been major European powers in the seventeenth.

7 Brinton, 'Introductory note', in *American Scandinavian Society*, p. 8.

8 Anne Newlands, *Canadian Art from its Beginnings to 2000*, Toronto, 2000, p. 136.

9 Hill, *The Group of Seven*, p. 48.

10 Hans Brummer, 'Ett skandinavisk perspektiv', in *Terre sauvage: Kanadensisk landskapsmåleri og Group of Seven*, exh. cat., National Gallery of Canada, Ottawa, 1999, p. 16.

11 Newlands, *Canadian Art from its Beginnings to 2000*, p. 136.

12 J.E.H. MacDonald, quoted in Hill, *The Group of Seven*, p. 48.

13 Brummer, 'Ett skandinavisk perspektiv', in *Terre sauvage*, p. 16.

14 Not every work illustrated here by way of comparison was included in the exhibition of 1912–13, but they all correspond in style and subject matter to items shown there.

15 Work by Gallen-Kallela was shown in 1915–16 at the Panama–Pacific International Exhibition in San Francisco, in 1916 at the Palace of Arts in San Francisco and in 1923–24 at a solo exhibition in the Art Institute of Chicago.

16 Brummer, 'Ett skandinavisk perspektiv', in *Terre sauvage*, p. 16.

17 Hill, *The Group of Seven*, p. 48.

18 Brinton, 'Introductory Note', in *American Scandinavian Society*, p. 25.

19 Barbara Novak, 'Scandinavia and America: A Shared "Look"', in *En ny värld: Amerianskt landskapsmåleri 1830–1900*, Gothenburg, 1987, p. 117.

20 Philip Conisbee, 'From afar', in *A Mirror of Nature: Nordic Landscape Painting 1840–1910*, exh. cat., Statens Museum for Kunst, Copenhagen, 2006, pp. 207–8.

21 Brummer, 'Ett skandinavisk perspektiv', in *Terre sauvage*, p. 17.

22 Novak, 'Scandinavia and America: A Shared "Look"', p. 116.

23 Torsten Gunnarsson, 'The New World and the Old: The relationship between American and European landscape painting in the 19th century', in *En ny värld*, p. 119.

24 Gunnarsson, 'The New World and the Old', p. 119.

25 Thomas Cole, *Essay on American Scenery* (1835) in Philip Conisbee, 'From afar', p. 207.

26 Jens Thiis, 'The art of Norway', in *American Scandinavian Society*, p. 45.

27 Brinton, 'Introductory note', in *American Scandinavian Society,* p. 16.

28 Ibid., pp. 14–15.

Terra Incognita
The Group of Seven and the European Expressionist Landscape Tradition

Mariëtta Jansen

Fig. 43
Tom Thomson
Sketch for
'The Jack Pine' (detail)
1916
Oil on wood panel
21 x 26.7 cm
RiverBrink Art Museum
Collection, Queenston,
Ontario, Canada

The work of Tom Thomson and the Group of Seven, which forms a significant part of Canada's cultural heritage, is essentially late impressionist in character, with traits of expressionism. And yet the Group shared the conviction that their art was not directly connected to the artistic developments of early twentieth-century Europe, but instead inspired by their direct contact with Canada's natural environment. Indeed, Lawren Harris believed it was more a case of Group members influencing one another, rather than their being influenced from outside.[1] This helps to explain the importance the Group of Seven artists attached to authenticity; their modernist landscapes expressed their desire to create a national art with a clear Canadian signature. Donald W. Buchanan, a specialist in Canadian painting, was later to profoundly refine this view, stating: 'But no one, surely least these men of the Group themselves, wished Canadian painting to settle down into a sort of landscape routine symbolizing nationalism.'[2]

The innovative manner in which these artists portrayed the magnificence of Canadian nature has parallels with the expressionist landscape tradition as it manifested itself in northern Europe on the eve of the First World War. The term expressionism' – a concept that serves as counterpart to

impressionism – was first used around 1910 to describe a generation of young German artists who used simplified shapes and intensified colours as a way to escape the confines of traditional painting.[3] With this European trend in mind, Thomson's powerful portrayal of nature – and in particular his countless oil sketches – can be seen as expressionistic. As raw responses to nature, they have a sheer emotive impact and his lively use of colour together with rhythmic shapes clearly chime with the expressionist ethos. Literature on Thomson and the Group of Seven, however, seldom considers this parallel.

Although Thomson himself may never have set foot in Europe, members of the Group were well aware of recent European developments in art, having attended European art academies before the First World War – Lawren Harris in Berlin and A. Y. Jackson in Paris. The latter also visited the Netherlands in 1909, where he would have encountered the atmospheric landscape art of the Hague School. Back in Canada, Hague School artists such as Jozef Israëls, Jan Hendrik Weissenbruch and Anton Mauve were particularly popular in the period 1885–1914.[4] Marta Hurdalek claims that 'Hague School paintings in Canadian private collections and the number of exhibitions

Fig. 44
Vincent van Gogh
Cypresses
1889
Oil on canvas
93.4 x 74 cm
Metropolitan Museum
of Art, New York, Rogers
Fund, 1949 (49.30)

organised in this country inevitably influenced a portion of the younger generation of local artists'.[5] Although traces of the grey-toned Hague School landscapes can be discerned in Jackson's early work, this was not to be an enduring love affair. In his autobiography *A Painter's Country* he writes in retrospect: 'The Montreal collectors had acquired Barbizon paintings … but when French art went impressionistic Montreal buyers dropped it … they played safe and bought Dutch paintings at high prices. The only artists they ignored was [sic] Van Gogh and later Mondrian, probably the most important Dutch painters of the past hundred years'.[6]

Given this statement, it is interesting to see that after his return to Canada in 1913, Jackson's art took a remarkable turn. Paintings such as *Terre Sauvage* from 1913, and later works such as *March Storm, Georgian Bay* (cat. 45) cannot be fully understood without reference to the range of innovations in painting which by then had taken hold in Europe, and which certainly bring to mind painters other than those of the Hague School.

The degree to which Thomson, to take an example, was influenced by Vincent van Gogh is not easily established yet sources do confirm that he was an admirer of the Dutch artist's work.[7] A number of Van Gogh's late works were first seen in North America during the famous 1913 Armory Show in New York. Although none of the Group of Seven saw this exhibition, Harris and J.E.H. MacDonald were certainly impressed by a Scandinavian art exhibition earlier that year in Buffalo and it seems safe to conclude that the legacy of Van Gogh had by then entered the collective consciousness of the Group.[8] Thomson's 1916 sketch for *The Jack Pine* (cat. 10), for instance, when compared with Van Gogh's *Cypresses* from 1889 (fig. 44), shows a remarkable affinity in subject matter, in terms of the liberally applied colour, the lively brush technique, and the dynamic way the landscape is addressed.

It was in his small *en plein air* oil sketches – of which he was to paint some 300 between 1912 and 1917 – that Thomson was most able to surrender himself to creative instinct. Through these he not only managed to powerfully depict the essence of Canadian landscape, but also to discover his identity as an artist. It is these sketches, much more than work painted later in the studio, that show kinship with European expressionism, as found, for example, in the work of Emil Nolde (fig. 45). The German artist's exuberant use of colour and spirited brush technique in *Herbstmeer V* (*Autumn Lake V*), of 1910, is echoed in Thomson's *Yellow Sunset* (cat. 31) from 1916, by way of its dynamic approach to nature and use of vibrant colour. We may again trace this path back to Van Gogh, for, by 1910, Nolde's practice had just gone through a major evolution, and he had arrived at the stage where his admiration for Van Gogh generated original imagery with landscape at its core.

Just prior to Thomson creating his most colourful and robustly painted oil sketches around 1915, a movement in Europe was taking off that aimed to bridge old painting and the new. In 1905, in Dresden, the artists' group Die Brücke was founded; it is now considered a cornerstone of northern European expressionism. This collective, which included Ernst Ludwig Kirchner,

Fig. 45
Emil Nolde
Herbstmeer V
(Autumn Sea V)
1910
Oil on rough canvas
62.5 x 78 cm
Neukirchen, Nolde,
Stiftung Seebüll

Fig. 46
**Karl Schmidt-
Rottluff**
Deichdurchbruch
**(Breach in the
Dyke)**
1910
Oil on canvas
76 x 84 cm
Brücke-Museum Berlin
(Inv. Nr. 64)

the long-established older forces. Everyone who
reproduces that which drives him to creation
with directness and authenticity belongs to us.[9]

Besides subjects such as the nude, portraiture
and the world of cabaret, landscape was an
important Die Brücke theme. Simplified shapes
and an expressive use of colour were means
towards visualising our experience of the sensation
of nature. Nolde and Schmidt-Rottluff, for
example, who were initially strongly influenced
by Van Gogh, often focused on raw, unspoilt
nature. Although members of Die Brücke would
often work together – painting out in the open,
for instance near Moritzburg – Schmidt-Rottluff
would frequently venture out on his own,
a practice that fed into his most innovative
and expressionist work. A wonderful example is
Deichdurchbruch (*Breach in the Dyke*), (fig. 46)
where in bright, unmixed colours and with a wild,
untamed brush he endows the landscape with a
powerful character of its own. Just a short while
later, in their own quest to push the boundaries
of traditional painting and forge a unique
Canadian style using modern stylistic devices,
the Group of Seven managed to capture the unique
qualities of the Canadian landscape. By engaging
with and expressing the landscape in this way –
and in creating a mode of expression that would
resonate with all who had experienced that
landscape – the art of Thomson and the Group
of Seven is a direct parallel of the expressionist
landscape tradition that brought about a seismic
shift in the development of art in Europe.

This was the period when expressionism
was springing up across Europe in many guises:
in 1918, in the Netherlands, a group of artists
calling themselves De Ploeg was formed in the
rather remote city of Groningen. Although initially
these artists did not adhere to a homogenised style
of painting, matters were to take a dramatic turn
due to an extraordinary coincidence. In 1920, one
of the members of De Ploeg, Jan Wiegers, travelled
to Davos in Switzerland to recover his health.
There he met Ernst Ludwig Kirchner, at one
time the most prominent leader of Die Brücke.
The artists not only became friends, but also

Karl Schmidt-Rottluf, Erich Heckel, Max Pechstein,
and for a brief time Emil Nolde, strove towards
new forms of expression in painting.

Initially, Brücke art was characterised by
impressionist, Jugendstil and Japonist influences,
with Van Gogh again serving as an important point
of reference. The direction of the Brücke artists,
however, was determined from the outset by their
vigorous aspiration to modernise painting in
Germany. The programme outlined by Kirchner
for Die Brücke declared as such:

*With faith in progress and in a new generation
of creators and spectators we call together all youth.
As youth, we carry the future and want to create for
ourselves freedom of life and of movements against*

Fig. 47
Jan Wiegers
**Landschap met
rode bomen
(Landscape with
red trees)**
c. 1922
Wax/oil on canvas
70 x 70 cm
Collection Stedelijk
Museum Amsterdam

entered into a lively artistic exchange with far-reaching consequences for De Ploeg. When in 1921 Wiegers returned to the Netherlands, his fresh enthusiasm for new possibilities in painting soon infected other De Ploeg artists. They began experimenting with bright and contrasting colours, strong shapes and deformations, and encaustic, a new painting technique involving wax. The art that evolved was heavily indebted to German expressionism and was primarily used in portraiture and landscapes.

It was thanks to the art created by De Ploeg – it would later be said – that the concept of a Groningen landscape arose.[10] Wiegers's *Landschap met rode bomen* (*Landscape with Red Trees*) (fig. 47), painted sometime around 1922, shows the observed world transformed into an expressionist vision based on personal experience, with a strong emphasis on flat surface, bright colours and tempestuous brushwork. This led to other De Ploeg artists, such as Jan Altink and Johan Dijkstra, further discovering the Groningen landscape and capturing it in paint. The wide, empty countryside offered them pictorial possibilities that fitted a new artistic idiom. As Dijkstra was later to write: 'The landscape of the Groningen countryside, until then terra incognita to art … where the trees bear witness to the wind … It was as if they clamoured to be painted at last'.[11] This in turn brings to mind an often quoted statement by Group of Seven artist Harris: 'We had commenced our great adventure. We lived in a continuous blaze of enthusiasm. We were at times very serious and concerned, at other times hilarious and carefree. Above all, we loved this country and loved exploring and painting it'.[12]

A comparison between Wiegers's *Landschap met rode bomen* and Varley's *Stormy Weather, Georgian Bay* (cat. 52) – and countless other examples besides – reveal the results of artistic exploration of new territory: these are masterpieces of landscape art, captured expressively and passionately. In general, this development can be considered to have had an important side-effect on the way landscape art from the early decades of the twentieth century is appreciated. Henk van Os

writes that 'painters of landscapes are not meant to paint what is considered beautiful – it is what they find beautiful that we learn to appreciate thanks to their work'.[13]

Although the work of the Group of Seven has remained more or less unknown in the Netherlands, this is not the first time that Canadian art has been shown there. In 1958, the Groninger Museum held an exhibition of post Second World War contemporary Canadian painting, where Buchanan wrote in the exhibition catalogue: 'These days, Canadian painting is no longer so closely connected to the country's nature as it used to be. The far reaches of the northern forest, the lakes edged by spruce and pines and the steep, rocky shores that so strongly fired the imagination of the nationalist Group of Seven three or four decades ago, no longer are such a major source of inspiration to Canadian Art as they use to be'. The exhibition showcased work from a generation of artists who – according to Buchanan – wondered whether 'anyone could create a Canadian style in this world of change'.[14] The Group of Seven most certainly made a major contribution towards creating a Canadian style in the period 1913–33. To just what extent this Canadian style was fed by mutual influence from within the Group itself, or by influence from their exposure to European artistic tradition and its new developments, is ripe for discussion.

Taking expressionism as a comprehensive phenomenon in art – spanning the regional and international – makes for an interesting area to explore, where strands of direct and indirect influence abound. The similarities so inherent to the art of the Group of Seven, Die Brücke, and De Ploeg in Groningen – and no doubt of others as well – reveal a like-minded approach.

Expressionism as *zeitgeist* gusted across Europe and beyond, taking root wherever fertile soil was to be found. It is significant that the modernist landscapes of Tom Thomson and the Group of Seven also fit the expressionist landscape tradition outlined here – producing work that moreover was archetypal, the first to give Canadian landscape art a clear-cut, unique identity.

Notes

1 Angela Nairne Grigor, *Arthur Lismer, Visionary Art Educator*, Montreal: McGill-Queen's University Press, 2002, pp. 57–58.

2 Donald W. Buchanan, 'The story of Canadian art', *Canadian Geographical Journal*, vol. 17, no. 6, 1938, p. 279.

3 Magdalena M. Moeller, 'De kunstenaars van de Brücke', in Magdalena M. Moeller and Mariëtta Jansen, eds., *Duits Expressionisme 1905–1913, Brücke-Museum Berlijn*, Groninger Museum/Brücke-Museum Berlin, exh. cat., Hirmer Verlag, 2009, pp. 7–15.

4 Marta H. Hurdalek, *The Hague School: Collecting in Canada at the Turn of the Century*, Art Gallery of Ontario, exh. cat., Toronto, 1983, pp. 23–24.

5 Hurdalek, *The Hague School*. Hurdalek writes: 'That another Canadian artist A.Y. Jackson was attracted to the Dutch themes is evident from his sketchbook (given to the National Gallery of Canada in 1976) dating from his trip to Holland in 1909. The sketchbook constitutes an important document, revealing the artist's early fascination with Dutch motifs – something he later renounced … Much further research needs to be done to fully assess the impact of the Hague School on early Canadian painting', p. 23.

6 A.Y. Jackson, *A Painter's Country: The Autobiography of A.Y. Jackson*, Toronto: Clarke, Irwin & Co. Ltd, 1958, pp. 14–15, quoted in Hurdalek, *The Hague School*, pp. 23–24.

7 Harold Town and David P. Silcox, *Tom Thomson: The Silence and the Storm*, 4th rev. edn, Toronto: Firefly Books, 2001, pp. 103–5.

8 Roald Nasgaard, *The Mystic North: Symbolist Landscape Painting in Northern Europe and North America, 1890–1940*, Toronto: University of Toronto Press, 1984, pp. 160–61; for further discussion of the impact of Scandinavian art upon the work of Thomson and the Group, see Nils Ohlsen's essay in this catalogue, pp. 47–53.

9 See Moeller, 'De kunstenaars van de Brücke', p. 8.

10 Henk W. van Os, *De Ploeg in Bergen: De keuze van Henk van Os uit drie particuliere collecties*, Museum Kranenburgh Bergen, cahier 7, Bergen, 1999, p. 17.

11 Johan Dijkstra, 'Een halve eeuw Ploeg', *Groningen Cultureel Maandblad*, vol. 10, 1968, p. 172.

12 Lawren Harris quoted in Peter Mellen, *The Group of Seven*, McClelland and Stewart, Toronto, 1970, p. 112.

13 Henk W. van Os, *De ontdekking van Nederland: vier eeuwen landschap verbeeld door Hollandse meesters* [The Discovery of the Netherlands: Four Centuries of Landscape as Depicted by Dutch Masters], Rotterdam: NAi Publishers, 2008, pp. 13–14.

14 Donald W. Buchanan, *Moderne Canadese schilderkunst*, Groningen: exh. cat., Groninger Museum, 12 December 1958 – 12 January 1959, 1958, p. 4.

Catalogue

Tom Thomson

It would be idle to pretend that the oils, large and very small (mostly the latter) produced by Thomson during a mere three years – 1914 to 1917 – which is all that is of interest, would set the Thames or the Seine on fire, because they would not.

Percy Wyndham Lewis[1]

Wyndham Lewis's interesting piece in *The Listener* (reproduced on pp. 203–5) is understandably biased in favour of A.Y. Jackson, whom he had met, and who was, at the date of writing (1946), the most accessible member of the original Group still working. Jackson was indeed an impressive painter of boundless energy, who loved travelling and who personified the 'artist with a rucksack' ideal. By 1946 Thomson was long dead, as was MacDonald, the oldest of the Group (he died in 1932). Carmichael, though the youngest of the original Group, had died in 1945, the year before Wyndham Lewis's article. Varley was more famous as a portraitist, Lismer a distinguished art educator. Harris was in Vancouver, painting abstracts. Johnston had broken his association with the Group very early on (he exhibited only once with the other members). Although Wyndham Lewis admitted that Thomson was a gifted colourist – albeit giving most of the credit for his becoming so to Jackson – he underestimated him, simply by judging him against European standards. If rivers were to be set on fire, they were not in Europe. However, he did put his finger on the most startling fact about Thomson, which was that he really has to be judged on the output of only three years, 1914 to 1917.

Thomson was born in 1877 on a farm in Claremont, east of Toronto, although he was brought up on the shores of Georgian Bay, at Leith. His family was Scottish in origin. Because of his untimely death he is forever frozen in the public consciousness as a young man, but had he lived he would have been one of the Group's elder statesmen – only MacDonald was older. However, he started painting late, in his thirties. His early life-story gave little inkling that he would become a famous artist, although his elder brother George also became a professional painter, having trained as a lawyer and then having run his own business school in Seattle. Although Tom started drawing at an early age, he had very little, if any, formal training and that was garnered at evening school. After spending some time at his brother's business school in Seattle, he found his way to Toronto, apparently exhibiting enough artistic talent to be taken on at Grip Ltd, a highly respected commercial engraving outfit, as a designer. His surviving output in this field seems workmanlike now, in the Arts and Crafts tradition, much influenced by Art Nouveau. However, Grip was effectively a haven for artists needing to make a living – Group members MacDonald, Lismer, Varley, Johnston and Carmichael all worked there at one time or another. He also benefited from the company policy of encouraging its artists to go forth (at weekends and holidays) and paint 'the real Canada' – a branding exercise that was to lead to Thomson's discovery of Algonquin Park, then a twelve-hour train journey north of Toronto.

Fig. 48
Tom Thomson
The Pointers (detail)
1916–17
Oil on canvas
101 x 114.6 cm
Hart House Permanent Collection, University of Toronto, purchase 1928–29

1 Percy Wyndham Lewis, 'Canadian nature and its painters', *The Listener*, vol. XXXVI, no. 920, 29 August 1946, pp. 267–68.

1

Tom Thomson
Burnt Country, Evening
1914
Oil on plywood
21.5 x 26.6 cm
National Gallery of Canada, Ottawa,
bequest of Dr J.M. MacCallum,
Toronto, 1944 (4661)

2

Tom Thomson
Burnt Land
1915
Oil on canvas
54.6 x 66.7 cm
National Gallery of Canada, Ottawa,
purchased 1937 (4299)

3

Tom Thomson
**Blue Lake, sketch for
'In the Northland'**
Autumn 1915
Oil on wood
21.7 x 26.9 cm
National Gallery of Canada, Ottawa,
bequest of Dr J.M. MacCallum,
Toronto, 1944 (4716)

4

Tom Thomson
Evening, Canoe Lake
Winter 1915–16
Oil on canvas
41.3 x 51.5 cm
The Thomson Collection,
Art Gallery of Ontario,
Toronto (69248)

5

Tom Thomson
Maple Woods, Bare Trunks
1915
Oil on wood
21.3 x 26.6 cm
National Gallery of Canada, Ottawa,
bequest of Dr J.M. MacCallum,
Toronto, 1944 (4682)

6

Tom Thomson
Maple Woods, Bare Trunks
Winter 1915–16
Oil on canvas
81 x 87 cm
Private collection

7

Tom Thomson
**The Opening of the Rivers,
sketch for 'Spring Ice'**
1915
Oil on composite wood-pulp board
21.6 x 26.7 cm
National Gallery of Canada, Ottawa,
bequest of Dr J.M. MacCallum, Toronto,
1944 (4662)

8

Tom Thomson
Spring Ice
1916
Oil on canvas
72 x 102.3 cm
National Gallery of Canada,
Ottawa (1195)

9
Tom Thomson
Sketch for 'The Jack Pine'
1916
Oil on wood panel
21 x 26.7 cm
RiverBrink Art Museum Collection,
Queenston, Ontario, Canada

10

Tom Thomson
The Jack Pine
1916
Oil on canvas
127.9 x 139.8 cm
National Gallery of Canada,
Ottawa, purchase 1918 (1519)

11

Tom Thomson
Sketch for 'The West Wind'
1916
Oil on composite wood board
21.4 x 26.8 cm
Art Gallery of Ontario, Toronto,
gift from the J.S. McLean Collection,
Toronto, 1969, donated by the
Ontario Heritage Foundation,
1988 (l.69.49)
Not exhibited

12

Tom Thomson
The West Wind
Winter 1916–17
Oil on canvas
120.7 x 137.9 cm
Art Gallery of Ontario, Toronto,
gift of the Canadian Club of
Toronto, 1926 (784)

13

Tom Thomson
The Pointers
1916–17
Oil on canvas
101 x 114.6 cm
Hart House Permanent Collection,
University of Toronto,
purchase 1928–29

14

**Tom Thomson's
Sketch Box**
Before 1913
Wood
6.5 x 30.5 x 27 cm
(closed including metal
fittings and leather handles)
National Gallery of Canada,
Ottawa (ST34)

Algonquin

Algonquin is Canada's oldest national park, established in 1893, north of Toronto and east of Georgian Bay. Its network of lakes, hills, streams and rapids, and its accessibility from Toronto and Ottawa by rail quickly established it as a resort for city-dwellers. But its landscape was also defined by the logging industry, which had briefly boomed in the 1890s (and still continues in a controlled fashion to this day). However, Mowat Lodge, where Thomson often stayed, in the vicinity of the Canoe Lake train station, was something of a ghost town, inhabited by only a handful of people, having once been the thriving hub of a major logging concern. The scars of logging were still everywhere and contributed much to the Park's appearance and atmosphere.

Thomson first visited the park in 1912. He was already thirty-four, had only very recently taken up landscape painting, and was effectively still a 'Sunday painter'. J.E.H. MacDonald had been the head of his section at Grip; MacDonald had already held an exhibition of his own work, and in 1912 'took the plunge' of leaving paid work to go freelance and hopefully become a full-time artist. His example (and active encouragement) no doubt made Thomson think, perhaps for the first time, that he could do something similar. The lakes and woods of Algonquin very quickly absorbed him, and he chose to spend more and more of his time there.

In Thomson's short period of artistic activity he was surprisingly prolific, particularly since he seems to have been just as interested in spending his time exploring by canoe – he managed some remarkable voyages – and in fishing, at which he was considered expert. A pattern emerged for the few years left to him: Thomson would head for Algonquin as soon as spring allowed, spend the summer exploring, camping, fishing and painting there, leave as the autumn weather closed in, and spend the winter back in Toronto working up a few of his sketches into finished canvases. In 1914, he briefly shared a studio with Jackson, then with Carmichael; but a shortage of funds eventually led to him adapting a wooden shack nearby for his purposes. When in Toronto, he lived and worked in what can be imagined as extremely primitive, not to mention freezing, conditions (the shack now stands as a kind

Fig. 49
Tom Thomson
Winter in the Woods (detail)
1916
Oil on wood
21.4 x 26.5 cm
National Gallery of Canada, Ottawa, bequest of Dr J.M. MacCallum, Toronto, 1944 (4655)

of national monument having been relocated to the grounds of the McMichael Canadian Art Collection in Kleinburg, Ontario). More finished works survive than one might expect, considering the difficulty of Thomson's circumstances and the limited time that he was prepared to spend developing his sketches. The process he went through of translating their freshness and immediacy into something fit for a gallery wall is always fascinating, and some of the end results are indeed masterly; but it was in the landscape sketch, 21 x 27 cm in size, that Thomson found his most electrifying and personal means of expression. The size of these small boards was dictated by practicality – they were readily available, and portable by canoe and backpack. Thomson, like the other Group of Seven artists, had a special sketching box (cat. 14) with slots that kept the boards apart to allow air to circulate round each finished sketch and protect the paint surface as it dried. Painting *en plein air* can rarely have been more taxing. This was not like Monet in a sun hat setting up his easel by the Seine. The box doubled as an easel and a palette, and was balanced on their knees (see figs. 50 and 51). The weather was often atrocious and in spring, when recording the breaking up of ice on the lakes (Spring Ice, cat. 8), and late autumn, conditions must have been almost unbearably cold. Furthermore, in Thomson's very last spring, 1917, he endured a particularly bad black fly season, while in 1912, after weeks of rain during his first major canoe trip, he lost most of his sketches and photographs when his canoe capsized in a forty-mile stretch of rapids towards the end of the journey.

Despite the apparent luminosity of Thomson's sketches, each one was usually carried out using a very limited selection of colours, three or four at most. Again, this is most likely a product of the difficulty of circumstances,

as is the evident speed with which they were produced. Limiting the colours to very few squeezes of paint from the tube at the outset of painting meant that Thomson was obliged to think in terms of colour as tone – and this was to be one of his greatest skills. Although notionally painted as sketches – preparatory to a 'finished' work – something about the process itself, perhaps even the limitations imposed on him, particularly suited him (as it suited James Dickson Innes over in Wales in 1912, working feverishly on small wooden panels against the ticking clock of developing tuberculosis); and he produced far more than he could possibly have hoped to work up later in the studio. He recorded whatever caught his eye – there would be time enough to pick out compositions suitable for developing back in Toronto over the winter. He seems not to have valued the sketches particularly. He was notoriously generous, giving away sketches – and money – at the drop of a hat, occasionally frustrating his friends who had a clearer idea of their value and felt he needed protecting from himself in this regard. Eventually, they took to trying to prevent visitors to Thomson's shack/studio in Toronto – the slightest expression of admiration by a visitor for a sketch was likely to lead to it being handed over on the spot. However, during the spring of 1917 he embarked upon a project to record methodically the onset of spring day by day in sketches. This perhaps indicates that Thomson had recognised the potential of the sketch in its own right, and may indeed even have begun to think of it as his most powerful creative tool.

The full-size finished canvases show Thomson grappling with some quite complex ideas for a painter of his limited experience, for instance in *The Pointers*, with its display of Post-Impressionist pointillism (cat. 13). *The Jack Pine* (cat. 10), on the other hand,

Fig. 50
J.E.H. MacDonald sitting with his easel/box open on his knee
c. 1918–19
National Gallery of Canada Archives

Fig. 51
**Franklin Carmichael
sketching at Grace Lake**
1935
McMichael Canadian Art
Collection Archives

uses a more block-like approach, building up strata of intense colour in horizontal formation (the ultimate inspiration for this may have been Gauguin). *The West Wind* (cat. 12) is different again, with decorative black outlines defining the pine tree. This is most reminiscent of Arthur Lismer, who is always notable for his strong graphic basis (the most powerful examples here being his *A September Gale, Georgian Bay* (cat. 48), and the almost brutal and cartoon-like *Evening Silhouette* (cat. 47), which takes Thomson's lone pine theme and pushes it to an expressionist extreme) and who shared sketching expeditions with Thomson. All three of these paintings by Thomson were produced in that last winter of 1916–17. It seems clear that Thomson was experimenting, putting into practice ideas that he had discussed with his fellow artists (he had never seen a Van Gogh – but Harris and Jackson, at least, certainly had), or seen in *Studio* magazine, or observed in other artists' work. While it cannot be said that he arrived at a definitive individual style, he was an exceptionally powerful image-maker (his only failures being those pictures which include people – he was no figure-painter). Some of them are among the most popular paintings ever produced in Canada; and his very first fully realised landscape painting, *Northern Lake*, sold to the government of the Province of Ontario. The artist David Milne summed him up as: '*the* Canadian painter, harsh, brilliant, brittle, uncouth, not only most Canadian but most creative. How the few things of his stick in one's mind'.[1]

Yet the full-size works essentially remain fascinating attempts to find a formal means of translating the immediacy of his sketches into a more finished article. Looking again at *The Pointers*, it is clear that the vivid stripe of cloud across the sky is a rationalisation, in pointillist dabs of colour, of a single sweep of wet paint in the original sketch. Similarly, the building blocks of horizontal dabs of colour that make up the lake and sky of *The Jack Pine* find no direct counterpart in the lush, stirred-in, swirls of the sketch – he has simply taken the overall tone and the composition, intensified the colours and laid them out according to a preconceived plan, emphasising the graphic impact of the design. Here, certainly, the end result may be said to have exceeded the power of the sketch. A particularly interesting example, in this regard, is the rarely seen work *Maple Woods, Bare Trunks* (cats. 5 and 6). Thomson's final canvas stays close to the feel of the sketch; in some ways the finished version reads like a sketch itself, but on a large scale.

As his friends came to terms with his death, it was his sketches that seemed to embody what was important about Thomson: his directness of vision. He looked at a bank of trees in snow, saw something special in it, and painted it in so vivid a way that the viewer seems to see the bank through Thomson's very own eyes, senses the exact quality of the light and even the time of day, and feels the bite in the air (see *Winter Thaw in the Woods*, cat. 37, for example). The sketches have the impact and force, for every viewer, of personal memory. Thomson's example elevated the oil sketch to a new level; as an exponent of this particular Canadian art form, he perhaps remains supreme. The entire Group did sketch in this way, but only MacDonald reaches similar heights. It is arguable that the Canadian oil sketch is these painters' greatest and most distinctive contribution to art.

1 Letter to H.O. McCurry of the National Gallery of Canada, quoted in David P. Silcox, *The Group of Seven and Tom Thomson*, Firefly Books, 2003, p. 20.

15

Tom Thomson
Moonlight
c. 1915
Oil on board
26.4 x 21.6 cm
Private collection

16

Tom Thomson
Moonlight and Birches
1915
Oil on wood panel
22 x 26.9 cm
McMichael Canadian Art Collection,
Kleinburg, Canada, gift of
Mrs H.P. de Pencier (1966.2.5)

17

Tom Thomson
Phantom Tent
1915
Oil on wood panel
21.4 x 26.7 cm
McMichael Canadian Art Collection,
Kleinburg, Canada, gift of
Mr R.A. Laidlaw (1969.2.3)

18

Tom Thomson
The Tent
1915
Oil on wood panel
21.5 x 26.8 cm
McMichael Canadian Art Collection,
Kleinburg, Canada, purchase
1979 (1979.18)

19

Tom Thomson
Tamaracks
1915
Oil on wood panel
21.3 x 26.7 cm
McMichael Canadian Art Collection,
Kleinburg, Canada, gift of
Mr R.A. Laidlaw (1968.12)

20

Tom Thomson
Tamarack
Autumn 1915
Oil on wood
21.5 x 26.2 cm
National Gallery of Canada,
Ottawa (1522)

21

Tom Thomson
Smoke Lake
1915
Oil on wood panel
21.5 x 26.9 cm
McMichael Canadian Art Collection,
Kleinburg, Canada, gift of
Mr and Mrs W.D. Patterson (1968.21)

22

Tom Thomson
Approaching Snowstorm
1915
Oil on wood
21.3 x 26.6 cm
National Gallery of Canada, Ottawa,
bequest of Dr J.M. MacCallum,
Toronto, 1944 (4689)

23

Tom Thomson
A Northern Lake
c. 1916
Oil on composite wood-pulp board
21.6 x 26.7 cm
Art Gallery of Ontario, Toronto, gift
from the Reuben and Kate Leonard
Canadian Fund, 1927 (848)

24

Tom Thomson
Potters Creek, Canoe Lake
c. 1916
Oil on wood panel
21.4 x 26.7 cm
Art Gallery of Ontario,
Toronto, gift from the estate of
R. Fraser Elliott, 2005 (2005/166)

25

Tom Thomson
Nocturne, The Birches
Spring 1916
Oil on composite wood-pulp board
21.6 x 26.8 cm
National Gallery of Canada, Ottawa,
bequest of Dr J.M. MacCallum,
Toronto, 1944 (4711)

26

Tom Thomson
Spring
1916
Oil on wood
21.2 x 26.7 cm
National Gallery of Canada, Ottawa,
bequest of Dr J.M. MacCallum,
Toronto, 1944 (4679)

27

Tom Thomson
March
1916
Oil on wood
26.9 x 21.4 cm
National Gallery of Canada, Ottawa,
bequest of Dr J.M. MacCallum,
Toronto, 1944 (4699)

28

Tom Thomson
Campfire
1916
Oil on wood
26.6 x 21.6 cm
National Gallery of Canada, Ottawa,
bequest of Dr J.M. MacCallum,
Toronto, 1944 (4646)

29

Tom Thomson
Ragged Oaks
1916
Oil on panel
21.5 x 26.7 cm
Private collection

30

Tom Thomson
Birches
1916
Oil on wood
21.3 x 26.7 cm
National Gallery of Canada,
Ottawa (1540)

31

Tom Thomson
Yellow Sunset
1916
Oil on wood
21.3 x 26.7 cm
National Gallery of Canada, Ottawa,
bequest of Dr J.M. MacCallum,
Toronto, 1944 (4684)

32

Tom Thomson
Purple Hill
1916
Oil on wood panel
21.6 x 26.7 cm
McMichael Canadian Art Collection,
Kleinburg, Canada, gift of
Mrs H.P. de Pencier (1966.2.4)

33

Tom Thomson
Winter in the Woods
1916
Oil on wood
21.4 x 26.5 cm
National Gallery of Canada, Ottawa,
bequest of Dr J.M. MacCallum,
Toronto, 1944 (4655)

34

Tom Thomson
Northern Lights
1916 or 1917
Oil on wood
21.5 x 26.7 cm
National Gallery of Canada, Ottawa,
bequest of Dr J.M. MacCallum,
Toronto, 1944 (4677r)

35

Tom Thomson
Birches
1917
Oil on wood panel
12.9 x 18.7 cm
McMichael Canadian Art Collection,
Kleinburg, Canada, purchase
1979 (1979.15)

36

Tom Thomson
Larry Dickson's Cabin
Spring 1917
Oil on wood
21.3 x 26.6 cm
National Gallery of Canada,
Ottawa (1528)

37

Tom Thomson
Winter Thaw in the Woods
Spring 1917
Oil on composite wood-pulp board
21.6 x 26.8 cm
The Thomson Collection,
Art Gallery of Ontario,
Toronto (69207)

38

Tom Thomson
Path Behind Mowat Lodge
Spring 1917
Oil on wood
26.8 x 21.4 cm
The Thomson Collection,
Art Gallery of Ontario,
Toronto (69219)

39

Tom Thomson
The Rapids
Spring 1917
Oil on wood panel
21.6 x 26.7 cm
Private collection

40

Tom Thomson
Spring in Algonquin Park
1917
Oil on wood panel
21.2 x 26.7 cm
McMichael Canadian Art Collection,
Kleinburg, Canada, purchase
1980 (1980.5)

41

Tom Thomson
Spring Flood
1917
Oil on wood panel
21.2 x 26.8 cm
McMichael Canadian Art Collection,
Kleinburg, Canada, gift of
Mr R.A. Laidlaw (1966.15.23)

42

Tom Thomson
Tea Lake Dam
1917
Oil on wood panel
21.3 x 26.2 cm
McMichael Canadian Art Collection,
Kleinburg, Canada, purchased with funds
donated by Mr R.A. Laidlaw (1970.1.4)

Georgian Bay

Georgian Bay is an enormous body of water making up the eastern side of Lake Huron, falling entirely within the province of Ontario. It has almost the character of a separate lake, comparable in size to Lake Ontario. It is notable for its astonishing number of islands, the 'Thirty Thousand Islands'.

Tom Thomson's early life was spent on the shores of Georgian Bay; and the area was to loom large for the artists of the Group of Seven, not least because their patron Dr MacCallum owned an island with a cottage on it at Go Home Bay. MacCallum was happy to entertain his artist friends here, or make it available to them when he was not there. A.Y. Jackson visited the area first upon relocating from Montreal to Toronto in 1914; he made good use of MacCallum's cottage and returned to the area often, referring to it as his 'happy hunting ground'.[1] Jackson loved its countless rocky islands (cat. 46, *Night, Pine Island*) and its vastness – the airy sweep of endless water and pine-strewn rocks, buffeted by winds. The spectacular storms that rattled the bay were an inspiration to its visiting artists. Jackson's *March Storm, Georgian Bay*

(cat. 45) captures a particularly cataclysmic onslaught of snowclouds over dark water. Arthur Lismer and Fred Varley painted virtually the same view (Lismer's sketch for *A September Gale*, cat. 49 and Varley's *Stormy Weather, Georgian Bay*, fig. 52, cat. 52). Varley's painting is one of the Group of Seven's greatest achievements, the wind whipping the foreground pine and churning the waters of the bay into a maelstrom of white water. The force of the wind is tangible, but the whole scene sparkles with brilliant sunlight. He achieves a similar effect in a sketch, *Sun and Wind, Georgian Bay* (cat. 50), this time at evening, and again in the sketch of *Peter Sandiford at Split Rock* (cat. 53). Lismer's two Georgian Bay canvases, *September Gale* and *Evening Silhouette* (cats. 49 and 48), illustrate very well this artist's adoption of a more graphic visual language, defined by strong shapes and dark outlines. His wind-blown pine in *Evening Silhouette* is a calligraphic gesture of almost Japanese effect; while *September Gale* clearly has Thomson's iconic *The West Wind* (cat. 12) in mind.

1 A.Y. Jackson, *A Painter's Country*, Clarke, Irwin & Co. Ltd., first published 1958, memorial edition 1976, p. 60.

Fig. 52
Frederick Horsman Varley
Stormy Weather,
Georgian Bay (detail)
1921
Oil on canvas
132.6 x 162.8 cm
National Gallery of Canada,
Ottawa (1814)

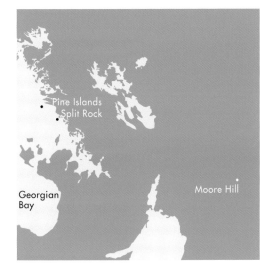

43

Tom Thomson
Pine Island
1914
Oil on paperboard
21.7 x 26.7 cm
McMichael Canadian Art Collection,
Kleinburg, Canada, gift of the Founders,
Robert and Signe McMichael (1966.16.70)

44

Tom Thomson
Evening, Pine Island
1914
Oil on panel
26.4 x 21.6 cm
Private collection

45

A.Y. Jackson
March Storm, Georgian Bay
1920
Oil on canvas
63.5 x 81.3 cm
National Gallery of Canada, Ottawa,
bequest of Dr J.M. MacCallum,
Toronto, 1944 (5051)

46

A.Y. Jackson
Night, Pine Island
1924
Oil on canvas
64.2 x 81.5 cm
National Gallery of Canada, Ottawa,
bequest of Dorothy Lampman McCurry,
1974, in memory of her husband
Harry O. McCurry, Director of the
National Gallery of Canada from
1939–1955 (18124)

47

Arthur Lismer
Evening Silhouette
c. 1926
Oil on board
32.6 x 40.7 cm
McMichael Canadian Art Collection,
Kleinburg, Canada, gift of the
Founders, Robert and Signe McMichael
(1966.16.108)

48

Arthur Lismer
Evening Silhouette
1928
Oil on canvas
80.3 x 100.8 cm
University College Collection, UC 286,
University of Toronto Art Centre,
Toronto, Ontario, Canada

49

Arthur Lismer
A September Gale, Georgian Bay
1921
Oil on panel
27.8 x 40.7 cm
Private collection

50

Frederick Horsman Varley
Sun and Wind, Georgian Bay
c. 1915
Oil on panel, mounted on plywood
31.1 x 41.2
Private collection

51

Frederick Horsman Varley
Squally Weather, Georgian Bay
1920
Oil on wood
30 x 40.9 cm
National Gallery of Canada, Ottawa,
gift of Mrs S.J. Williams, Mrs Harvey Sims,
Mrs T.M. Cram, and Miss Geneva Jackson,
Kitchener, Ontario, 1943 (4582)

52

Frederick Horsman Varley
**Stormy Weather,
Georgian Bay**
1921
Oil on canvas
132.6 x 162.8 cm
National Gallery of Canada,
Ottawa (1814)

53

Frederick Horsman Varley
Peter Sandiford at Split Rock,
Georgian Bay
1922
Oil on wood panel
21 x 26.7 cm
Art Gallery of Ontario, Toronto,
gift in memory of Dr Martin Baldwin
by the Art Institute of Ontario, 1968 (68/5)

54

J.E.H. MacDonald
Moore Hill, Gull River
c. 1921
Oil on board
21.3 x 26.4 cm
Art Gallery of Ontario, Toronto,
gift from the Fund of the T. Eaton Co. Ltd.
for Canadian Works of Art, 1959 (50/16)

Southern Ontario and Algoma

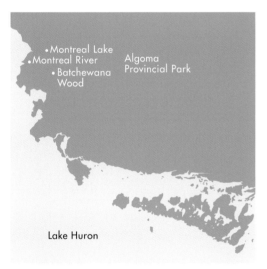

Fig. 53
Frank Johnston
Algoma Arabesque
(detail)
1924
Tempera on paper
55 x 58.5 cm
Private collection

There were other picturesque subjects for artists in southern Ontario within relatively easy reach of Toronto. Indeed, *Lansing*, painted by Franklin Carmichael (cat. 57) is now within the city suburbs. However, it was the landscape further north that was to provide the next major source of inspiration for many of the Group.

Algoma, the area in the province of Ontario that stretches north from the north shore of Lake Huron and the north-east shore of Lake Superior, consisted of vast tracts of virtually uninhabited and varied scenery. It was accessible to artists only by means of the Algoma Central Railway. Consequently Lawren Harris, with millionaire aplomb, had a boxcar fitted up to be parked strategically in sidings as a base from which he and his friends could paint.

The area proved a valuable alternative to Algonquin Park for Harris, Jackson, MacDonald, Johnston and Lismer in the aftermath of Thomson's death and the end of the First World War. Its hills and huge areas of forest, peppered with tumbling streams, waterfalls and enclosed lakes provided a breadth and variety of subject matter that amounted to an opening-out of themes seen in simpler forms at Algonquin. Its lakes seemed deeper and more mysterious, with steep, timber-covered slopes that dazzled in autumn, inspiring MacDonald to produce one of his masterpieces, *October Shower Gleam* (cats. 77 and 78), where the last flourishes

of autumn colour are trapped in livid low light between black sky and the even blacker lake – the oppressive effect in the sketch is particularly striking. A similar air of breathless calm and mystery pervades his famous *Beaver Dam* (cat. 70). The area's hills allowed the artists to take full advantage of striking viewpoints: A.Y. Jackson's *First Snow, Algoma* (cat. 61) and another MacDonald masterpiece, *Falls, Montreal River* (cat. 79), are both painted from high up looking down, in Jackson's case across a sea of autumnal shades just as the first flurries of snow start, and in MacDonald's down a torrent tumbling through woodlands to a distant river.

Some of MacDonald's most striking sketches were made in Algoma, several with a boldness of colour never matched even by Thomson. He loved the intricate tapestry effect of leaves against rock and stream (*Woodland Brook, Algoma*, cat. 67 and *Autumn Leaves, Batchewana Wood, Algoma*, cat. 71) and the passages of intense colour reflected in still (*Beaver Dam and Birches*, cat. 68) or fast-moving water (*The Little Falls*, cat. 66). Lawren Harris produced some equally distinguished sketches in Algoma, but somehow that most individual of artists looks unlike himself in this setting – in fact, he looks like MacDonald (Harris, *Trees and Pool*, cat. 60) or even Johnston (Harris, *Tamaracks and Blue Hill*, cat. 59). The latter artist was in his element, as the intricate patterns of leaves and grasses suited his more decorative style (*Algoma Arabesque*, fig. 53, cat. 65).

55

Franklin Carmichael
Autumn Hillside
1920
Oil on canvas
76 x 91.4 cm
Art Gallery of Ontario, Toronto,
gift from the J.S. McLean Collection,
Toronto, 1969; donated by the Ontario
Heritage Foundation, 1988 (L69.16)

56

Franklin Carmichael
**Autumn Foliage
against Grey Rock**
c. 1920
Oil on wood-pulp board
25.2 x 30.5 cm
National Gallery of Canada,
Ottawa, gift of Mary Mastin,
Toronto, 1996 (38405)

57

Franklin Carmichael
Lansing
c. 1921
Oil on paperboard
30.3 x 24.7 cm
McMichael Canadian Art Collection,
Kleinburg, Canada, purchase 1987 (1987.9)

58

Franklin Carmichael
October Gold
1922
Oil on canvas
119.5 x 98 cm
McMichael Canadian Art Collection,
Kleinburg, Canada, gift of the Founders,
Robert and Signe McMichael (1966.16.1)

59

Lawren Harris
Tamaracks and Blue Hill
Oil on panel
c. 1919
26.7 x 34.7 cm
Art Gallery of Ontario, Toronto, gift from
the Fund of the T. Eaton Co. Ltd. for
Canadian Works of Art, 1951 (50/60)

60

Lawren Harris
Trees and Pool
c. 1920
Oil on panel
26.7 x 35.6 cm
Art Gallery of Ontario, Toronto,
gift from the Friends of Canadian
Art Fund, 1938 (2465)

61

A.Y. Jackson
First Snow, Algoma
c. 1919–20
Oil on canvas
107.1 x 127.7 cm
McMichael Canadian Art Collection,
Kleinburg, Canada, in memory of
Gertrude Wells Hilborn (1966.7)

62

Frank Johnston
The Fire Ranger
1921
Oil on canvas
123 x 153.2 cm
National Gallery of Canada,
Ottawa (1823)

63

Frank Johnston
**Serenity (Distant Kenora),
Lake of the Woods**
1922
Oil on canvas
26.3 x 32.5 cm
Private collection

64

Frank Johnston
Serenity, Lake of the Woods
1922
Oil on canvas
102.3 x 128.4 cm
Collection of the Winnipeg Art
Gallery (L-102)

65

Frank Johnston
Algoma Arabesque
1924
Tempera on paper
55 x 58.5 cm
Private collection

66

J.E.H. MacDonald
The Little Falls
1918
Oil on composite wood board
21.6 x 26.7 cm
Art Gallery of Ontario, Toronto,
purchase, 1933 (2106)

67

J.E.H. MacDonald
Woodland Brook, Algoma
1918
Oil on board
21.6 x 26.7 cm
McMichael Canadian Art Collection,
Kleinburg, Canada, gift of the Founders,
Robert and Signe McMichael (1966.16.31)

68

J.E.H. MacDonald
Beaver Dam and Birches
c. 1919
Oil on wood panel
21.5 x 26.4 cm
McMichael Canadian Art Collection,
Kleinburg, Canada, gift of the Founders,
Robert and Signe McMichael (1966.16.49)

69

J.E.H. MacDonald
Beaver Dam
September 1919
Oil on board
21.2 x 26.7 cm
Collection of the Faculty Club,
University of Toronto

70

J.E.H. MacDonald
The Beaver Dam
1919
Oil on canvas
81.6 x 86.7 cm
Art Gallery of Ontario,
Toronto, gift from
the Reuben and Kate Leonard
Canadian Fund, 1927 (840)

71

J.E.H. MacDonald
Autumn Leaves,
Batchewana Wood, Algoma
c. 1919
Oil on composite wood board
21.6 x 26.7 cm
Art Gallery of Ontario, Toronto,
gift of the Students' Club, Ontario
College of Art, Toronto, 1933 (2115)

72

J.E.H. MacDonald
Near Montreal Lake, Algoma
1919
Oil on cardboard
21.6 x 26.5 cm
National Gallery of Canada,
Ottawa (15496)

73

J.E.H. MacDonald
Autumn Bush, Algoma
c. 1919–20
Oil on wood pulp board
21.3 x 26.6 cm
National Gallery of Canada,
Ottawa (4986)

74

J.E.H. MacDonald
Algoma Hills
1920
Oil on paperboard
21.4 x 26.4 cm
McMichael Canadian Art Collection,
Kleinburg, Canada, gift of
Mr R.A. Laidlaw (1966.15.6)

75

J.E.H. MacDonald
Mist Fantasy, Sand River, Algoma
1920
Oil on cardboard
21.4 x 26.6 cm
National Gallery of Canada,
Ottawa (4858)

76

J.E.H. MacDonald
Mongoose Lake, Algoma
1920
Oil on wood pulp board
21.4 x 26.5 cm
National Gallery of Canada,
Ottawa (4854)

77

J.E.H. MacDonald
**Sketch for October
Shower Gleam**
c. 1922
Oil on paperboard
21.6 x 26.7 cm
The Thomson Collection,
Art Gallery of Ontario,
Toronto (103882)

78

J.E.H. MacDonald
October Shower Gleam
1922
Oil on canvas
105.4 x 120.7 cm
Hart House Permanent Collection,
University of Toronto

79

J.E.H. MacDonald
Falls, Montreal River
1920
Oil on canvas
121.9 x 153 cm
Art Gallery of Ontario, Toronto,
purchase 1933 (2109)

80

Frederick Horsman Varley
Autumn Prelude
1938
Oil on canvas
55.4 x 70.9 cm
The Thomson Collection,
Art Gallery of Ontario,
Toronto (108065)

Quebec

The huge province of Quebec borders Ontario to the west, but stretches right up to the Hudson Strait, with Hudson Bay forming part of its north-western border, and reaches right down to the edge of New York State to the south. Of particular interest to artists was the country just north of the cities of Montreal and Quebec, especially the gentle landscape of the Laurentian Hills.

Quebec had always provided ample subject matter for artists, including an early work by MacDonald, *Laurentian Hillside, October* (cat. 86). But this was A.Y. Jackson's country; Montreal was home, and he preferred to spend his winters in Quebec even after he had made his move to Toronto. Montreal had its own art scene, frustration with which

was one of the factors that drove Jackson to Toronto in the first place. Nonetheless, during his winter sojourns he developed a special brand of poetic Quebecois landscape, very often winter or early spring scenes in rural communities, with the vernacular architecture of farms (cat. 84) and villages (cat. 81). In these subjects he created his own brand of quiet picturesque, very different from the developing subject matter of the rest of the Group. Recording the unique (and, as he keenly felt, fast disappearing) culture of the French-speaking province (*Le Calvaire or Wayside Cross, Saint-Urbain*, cat. 83) gave Jackson a spiritual platform from which to launch his energetic pursuit of new territories to conquer (with the paintbrush) during the summertime.

Fig. 54
A.Y. Jackson
Winter, Quebec (detail)
1926
Oil on canvas
53.8 x 66.5 cm
National Gallery of Canada,
Ottawa, Vincent Massey Bequest,
1968 (15482)

81

A.Y. Jackson
Early Spring, Quebec
c. 1923
Oil on canvas
54 x 66.6 cm
National Gallery of Canada,
Ottawa, purchased 1926 (3349)

82

A.Y. Jackson
Winter, Quebec
1926
Oil on canvas
53.8 x 66.5 cm
National Gallery of Canada,
Ottawa, Vincent Massey Bequest,
1968 (15482)

83

A.Y. Jackson
Le Calvaire or
Wayside Cross,
Saint-Urbain
1929
Oil on canvas
53.3 x 66 cm
Private collection

84

A.Y. Jackson
A Quebec Farm
c. 1930
Oil on canvas
82 x 102.3 cm
National Gallery of Canada,
Ottawa, Vincent Massey Bequest,
1968 (15481)

85

J.E.H. MacDonald
Laurentian Hillside
1913
Oil on cardboard
15 x 20 cm
Private collection

86

J.E.H. MacDonald
Laurentian Hillside, October
1914
Oil on canvas
75 x 100 cm
Private collection

The Canadian Rockies and British Columbia

As the Group spread out even further through Canada, it was not surprising that they should find inspiration in the Canadian Rockies. MacDonald spent his summers there from 1924; and the awe-inspiring mountains and lakes of the region brought on a shift in style comparable to that provoked in Lawren Harris by the austerity of Lake Superior's north shore. His richness of colour remained, but in works like *Lake O'Hara* (cat. 89) the forms are simplified into flat planes; and in *Dark Autumn, Rocky Mountains* (fig. 55, cat. 94) he has formalised the sky into a dense repeating pattern. Harris, Lismer and Jackson all painted in the Rockies, but it remains very much MacDonald's special place.

In 1926, Fred Varley moved to Vancouver, British Columbia, to teach; Lawren Harris would eventually move that way too. Although primarily interested in portraiture, Varley painted a steady stream of landscapes while there, reflecting the beautiful but very different scenery of the far west of Canada. These landscapes are highly individual, painterly in their brushwork and often exceptionally bold in colour – *West Coast Sunset, Vancouver* (cat. 92) mixes intense emeralds with bright blues and pinks to almost *fauve* effect, sometimes reminiscent of Emil Nolde. It was the mountains and coastline that caught his eye, rather than the forests that found their own artist in the remarkable Emily Carr. The two mountain pieces – *Cloud, Red Mountain* (cat. 96) and *Coast Mountain Form* (cat. 97) – use intensity of colour to suggest distance, eradicating foreground detail.

Fig. 55
J.E.H. MacDonald
Dark Autumn,
Rocky Mountains (detail)
1930
Oil on canvas
53.7 x 66.3 cm
National Gallery of Canada,
Ottawa, purchased 1948 (4875)

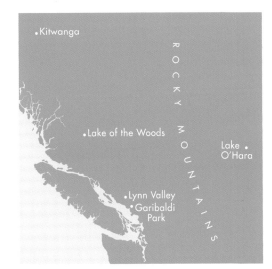

87

A.Y. Jackson
Totem Poles, Kitwanga
1926
Oil on panel
21.3 x 26.3 cm
Collection: A.K. Prakash
Exhibited only in London and Oslo

88

J.E.H. MacDonald
Lake McArthur,
Lake O'Hara Camp
c. 1924
Oil on paperboard
21.6 x 26.7 cm
McMichael Canadian Art Collection,
Kleinburg, Canada, gift of
Mr C.A.G. Matthews (1968.25.18)

89

J.E.H. MacDonald
Lake O'Hara
1925
Oil on hardboard
22.2 x 27.4 cm
Collection of the Winnipeg Art Gallery,
gift from the Estate of
Arnold O. Brigden (G-73-281)

90

J.E.H. MacDonald
Cathedral Mountain
1927
Oil on paperboard
21.4 x 26.6 cm
McMichael Canadian Art Collection,
Kleinburg, Canada, gift
of Mr R.A. Laidlaw (1966.15.8)

91

J.E.H. MacDonald
Waterfall near Lake O'Hara
1929
Oil on composite wood board
21.5 x 26.7 cm
Art Gallery of Ontario, Toronto,
gift of the Students' Club, Ontario
College of Art, Toronto, 1933 (2114)

92

J.E.H. MacDonald
Mount Biddle
Oil on composite wood board
1930
21.5 x 26.7 cm
Art Gallery of Ontario, Toronto,
gift from the Fund of the T. Eaton
Co. Ltd. For Canadian Works of Art,
1953 (52/53)

93

J.E.H. MacDonald
Lake O'Hara
1930
Oil on canvas
53.6 x 66.5 cm
The Thomson Collection,
Art Gallery of Ontario,
Toronto (2004/8)

94

J.E.H. MacDonald
**Dark Autumn,
Rocky Mountains**
1930
Oil on canvas
53.7 x 66.3 cm
National Gallery of Canada,
Ottawa, purchased 1948 (4875)

95

J.E.H. MacDonald
Snow at Lake Oesa
c. 1930
Oil on board
21.6 x 26.7 cm
Art Gallery of Ontario, Toronto,
gift of the Students' Club, Ontario
College of Art, Toronto, 1933 (2116)

96

J.E.H. MacDonald
Mountain Solitude (Lake Oesa)
1932
Oil on canvas
50.4 x 66.7 cm
Art Gallery of Ontario, Toronto,
gift of Stephen and Sylvia Morley,
in memory of Priscilla Bond Morley,
1995 (95/160)

97

J.E.H. MacDonald
Mount Oderay, Rockies
1930
Oil on canvas
40 x 52.5 cm
Collection: A.K. Prakash
Exhibited only in London and Oslo

98

Frederick Horsman Varley
West Coast Sunset, Vancouver
c. 1926
Oil on wood
30.4 x 38.1 cm
The Thomson Collection,
Art Gallery of Ontario,
Toronto (103850)

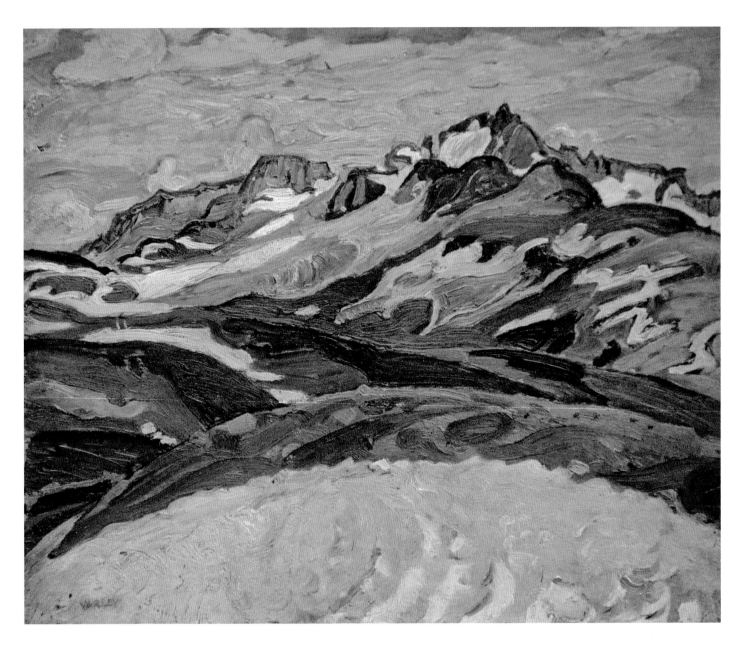

99

Frederick Horsman Varley
Snow in the Mountains, Garibaldi Park
1927
Oil on board
30 x 37.5 cm
Private collection

100

Frederick Horsman Varley
The Cloud, Red Mountain
1927–28
Oil on canvas
87 x 102.2 cm
Art Gallery of Ontario, Toronto,
bequest of Charles S. Band, Toronto,
1970 (69/127)

101

Frederick Horsman Varley
Coast Mountain Form
c. 1929
Oil on plywood
30.2 x 37.8 cm
National Gallery of Canada,
Ottawa, gift of Carolyn Morris,
Ottawa, 1952 (6119)

102

Frederick Horsman Varley
Lynn Valley
c. 1932–35
Oil on canvas board
50.8 x 61 cm
Private collection

Lawren Harris: Lake Superior, North Shore, Rockies and Arctic

Fig. 56
Lawren Harris
Grounded Icebergs
(Disco Bay) (detail)
c. 1931
Oil on canvas
80.0 x 101.6 cm
Art Gallery of Ontario,
Toronto, gift from the estate
of R. Fraser Elliott, 2005
(2005/156)

From Algoma, the Canadian Pacific Railway followed the north shore of Lake Superior, from Heron Bay to Port Arthur. Harris and Jackson, and later Carmichael, found the landscape impressive and inspiring. The vast lake, with its sweeping ranges of rounded hills, burnt clear of undergrowth, and its grand islands such as Pic Island (cats. 111 and 112), provided a sense of scale and a wildness that was unmatched in Canada. There were few places to stay, so camping was essential. Here Harris found the inspiration that led to his later style, pared down to the bare bones. There was something huge and perfect about the rounded hills and hump-backed islands and the burnt stumps of trees became, in his paintings (cat. 108 and 109), and even in Carmichael's (cat. 106), seemingly loaded with symbolism. For Harris, and arguably for the others too, the defining development of the Group of Seven was away from the intimacy of Thomson's Algonquin towards a grander vision; away from leaves and trees to endless horizons and enormous skies. Harris's *From the North Shore, Lake Superior* (cat. 113) is one of his most beautiful paintings, an endless vista with bright light bursting through clouds onto the reflective surface of the lake below, a necklace of brighter clouds in flower-like forms strung across the middle of the composition.

This aesthetic journey coincided for the most part with a geographical one, with the artists travelling ever further west, east and north (but not south). The broadening of their landscapes reflected the actual broadening of their horizons; in some ways, the story of the Group of Seven is a travelogue. The north shore of Lake Superior provided Harris with the first of his revelatory spiritual landscapes, on his way to the Arctic, but Harris joined MacDonald in his enthusiasm for the majestic forms of the Rockies, such as Mount Lefroy (cats. 117–120).

It was Jackson who first travelled to the Arctic, in 1927, to be joined by Harris three years later with the support of the Canadian government. But it was Harris who discovered there some of his most majestic subject matter. In the icebergs of the Davis Strait (cat. 122) and Disco Bay (fig. 56, cat. 124), Harris found natural forms of unearthly beauty that suited his spiritual leanings – just sea, sky and ice, sculpted into astonishing shapes, these paintings represent the end of his journey with the Group of Seven. Not long after the Group disbanded, in 1934, Harris left his wife for Bess Housser, the wife of the Group's first biographer. The scandal was such that he felt he had to leave Canada for the States. By the time he returned, to Vancouver in 1940, he had entered a new phase of his career, as an abstract painter.

103

Franklin Carmichael
A Grey Day
1928
Oil on beaverboard
25.5 x 30.2 cm
National Gallery of Canada,
Ottawa, gift of Mary Mastin,
Toronto, 1996 (38411)

104

Franklin Carmichael
Port Coldwell (I)
1928
Oil on wood-pulp board
25.5 x 30.2 cm
National Gallery of Canada,
Ottawa, gift of Mary Mastin,
Toronto, 1996 (38407)

105

Franklin Carmichael
Grace Lake
1931
Oil on paperboard
25.4 x 30.4 cm
National Gallery of Canada,
Ottawa, purchased 1956 (6450)

106

Franklin Carmichael
Grace Lake
1931
Oil on canvas
101.6 x 122 cm
University College Collection, UC 084,
University of Toronto Art Centre, Toronto,
Ontario, Canada

107

Lawren Harris
Winter
1914
Oil on panel
25.9 x 33.1 cm
Collection: A.K. Prakash
Exhibited only in London and Oslo

108

Lawren Harris
Lake Superior Sketch VIII
c. 1923
Oil on panel
30 x 37.5 cm
Collection: A.K. Prakash
Exhibited only in London and Oslo

109

Lawren Harris
Lake Superior Sketch XXXIX
c. 1923
Oil on pulpboard
30.5 x 38.1 cm
Art Gallery of Ontario, Toronto,
gift from the Friends of
Canadian Art Fund, 1938 (2462)

110

Lawren Harris
Lake Superior Sketch XLVII
c. 1923
Oil on panel
30 x 37.5 cm
Collection: A.K. Prakash
Exhibited only in London and Oslo

111

Lawren Harris
Lake Superior (Pic Island)
c. 1923–24
Oil on paperboard
30.5 x 38.1 cm
Private collection

112

Lawren Harris
Lake Superior Island
c. 1923
Oil on canvas
74.2 x 89 cm
McMichael Canadian Art Collection,
Kleinburg, Canada, gift of
Mrs F.B. Housser (1966.5.3)

113

Lawren Harris
**From the North Shore,
Lake Superior**
c. 1927
Oil on canvas
121.9 x 152.4 cm
Collection of Museum London,
Ontario, gift of H.S. Southam Esq.,
Ottawa, Ontario, 1940

114

Lawren Harris
Untitled Mountain
Landscape
c. 1927–28
Oil on canvas
122.3 x 152.7 cm
The Thomson Collection,
Art Gallery of Ontario,
Toronto (103935)

115

Lawren Harris
Isolation Peak
c. 1929
Oil on panel
30 x 37.5 cm
Collection: A.K. Prakash
Exhibited only in London and Oslo

116

Lawren Harris
Isolation Peak
1930
106.7 x 127 cm
Hart House Permanent Collection,
University of Toronto

117

Lawren Harris
Mount Lefroy
c. 1925
Oil on wood panel
30.2 x 37.5 cm
McMichael Canadian Art Collection,
Kleinburg, Canada,
purchase 1986 (1986.1)

118

Lawren Harris
Rocky Mountain Sketch,
Mt. Lefroy
c. 1929
Oil on wood panel
30.5 x 38.1 cm
McMichael Canadian Art Collection,
Kleinburg, Canada, gift of
Mr R.G. Colgrove (1971.12)

119

Lawren Harris
Mt. Lefroy
c. 1929
Oil on wood panel
30.5 x 38.1 cm
McMichael Canadian Art Collection,
Kleinburg, Canada,
purchase 1973 (1981.85.2)

120

Lawren Harris
Mt. Lefroy
1930
Oil on canvas
133.5 x 153.5 cm
McMichael Canadian Art Collection,
Kleinburg, Canada,
purchase 1975 (1975.7)

121

Lawren Harris
Icebergs, Davis Strait
1930
Oil on panel
30.5 x 38.1 cm
Private collection

122

Lawren Harris
Icebergs, Davis Strait
1930
Oil on canvas
121.9 x 152.4 cm
McMichael Canadian Art Collection,
Kleinburg, Canada, gift of
Mr and Mrs H. Spencer Clark (1971.17)

123

Lawren Harris
**Albert Harbour,
North Baffin Island**
1930
Oil on panel
25.9 x 33.1 cm
Collection: A.K. Prakash
Exhibited only in London and Oslo

124

Lawren Harris
Grounded Icebergs
(Disco Bay)
c. 1931
Oil on canvas
80.0 x 101.6 cm
Art Gallery of Ontario,
Toronto, gift from the estate
of R. Fraser Elliott, 2005 (2005/156)

Canadian Nature and its Painters

Wyndham Lewis

This essay appeared in *The Listener*, vol. XXXVI, no. 920, 29 August 1946, pp. 267–68.
© By kind permission of the Wyndham Lewis Memorial Trust (a registered charity)

The Canadian consciousness must always, to a peculiar degree, be implicated with nature, seeing that Canada is first and foremost an agricultural and raw material nation, and, still more important, is everywhere on the frontiers of the wilderness.

The development of the cultural life of Canada will necessarily be conditioned – or so it seems to me – by these facts, however much present day anti-regionalism there may seek to ignore them. On the other hand its situation on the North American continent also deeply involves it in the Machine Age. The neighbourhood of Chicago and of Detroit is a formidable fact. The culture of this northernmost of the nations of the western hemisphere might develop, consequently, a dual personality. The pull of nature, however, will probably exceed that of the attraction exercised by the blast-furnace and power-house. Further, the Anglo-Saxon genius has always displayed great affinity with primitive nature. The French Canadian would, after his Latin fashion, continue no doubt to take more interest in man than in primitive nature. The latter is really, in practice if not in theory, and in spite of Rousseau and his school, almost an English monopoly.

An Ossianic pantheism pervades the literature and the life of the Briton: a passionate inclination for the virginity of nature and for the most unruly moods of the elements. Evidences of this can be traced as much in the fondness of Shakespeare for thunder and lightning, as in the appetite of a twentieth-century boy scout for getting lost on quite mild little mountains and practising woodcraft in the home-spinney.

These are the things however that have spelled Empire: that 'violent trading' of the English, as a Frenchman has called it, which eventuated in the North American continent speaking the English tongue: resulted in Hudson Bay, Ellesmere Land, Prince Patrick Island, and other cosy little spots, bearing Anglo-Saxon names, rather than Spanish, French, German, Italian, or Dutch. Such reflections are appropriate in approaching the question of what kind of culture may be produced by the population settled in such close neighbourhood to so overpowering and top-heavy a mass of primitiveness as is to be found in Canada, north of the narrow settled belt – from the Bush up to the muskeg and beyond to the icepack.

The question in fact is whether all this un-assimilable mass of 'nature' will in the end be left severely alone (just as we seldom turn our eyes up towards interstellar space, and have long ago lost interest in the moon, except for crooning

Fig. 57
A.Y. Jackson
Le Calvaire or Wayside Cross, Saint-Urbain (detail)
1929
Oil on canvas
53.3 x 66 cm
Private collection

purposes): or whether this proximity of the wilds will continue to influence the descendants of the contemporary Canadian. Surely the latter.

That I think is the answer; just as certainly as a people who inhabit a sea coast are conditioned by the neighbouring ocean and its rude habits – the works of their bards being full of splashing and tossing, of shipwreck and of ships inopportunely becalmed.

Now it seems to me that for a person with these tastes, and with these traditions, Canada, artistically, offers extraordinary opportunities, and that these have on the whole been surprisingly neglected. One would have expected for instance Canada to have produced one outstanding poet, inspired by the scene and by the history that is there; as native as the folk-song 'Alouette'. This has not occurred.

But pictorially, in a sense, it has. And the Phaidon Press publication, *Canadian Painters*, in its massed photographs, gives one an excellent idea of this flowering – though the effect is perhaps cartographical rather than horticultural. This painting is, in fact, the blazing of a trail and a rough charting – a sometimes crude advertisement of a rich aesthetic vein – rather than a finished achievement of authentic beauty.

In 1920 a movement announced itself in Upper Canada (that is English Canada) under the name of 'The Group of Seven'. This Phaidon volume celebrates the work of that group. A further volume is announced dealing with work reflecting contemporary European and American influences: for Canada on the whole, it could be said, is busy de-Canadianising itself, and firmly shutting the door upon the doctrinal 'regionalism' represented by the seven pioneers of post-war No. 1.

The key-man in this Canadian regionalist school is Alec Jackson, because without him it is doubtful if it would ever have existed. Tom Thomson, generally regarded as the star-member of the school, died, in mysterious circumstances up in one of his Northland lakes, in 1917. He was a commercial designer – as all of them were at one time or another, except Harris. In 1913–14

Thomson, then a week-end artist of no particular distinction, became acquainted with Jackson, not long returned from Paris, and a spark was struck. They shared a studio, and by the end of 1914 this contact had transformed Thomson into a remarkable colourist, equipped to get on to his canvas some of the cold vivacious beauty of the spring woods in the Algonquin country. For the rest, his ten years of commercial designing at Grip Limited supplied the formal accessories and the organising habit.

It would be idle to pretend that the oils, large and very small (mostly the latter) produced by Thomson during a mere three years – 1914 to 1917 – which is all that is of interest, would set the Thames or the Seine on fire, because they would not. Most gallantly this little group (for the rigors of the social climate were so formidable that only the toughest could survive) pioneered: when the hostility of the press and public held them up, they retreated into commercial design, but always to emerge again as – for the time and place – militant and iconoclastic. Their work was rude: they chopped out their paintings as if they had been chopping wood. They adopted, often, the brutal methods of the bill-board artist to put their country across big and harsh and plain: with all its emptiness and savagery – its trees that crawl along the surface of the frozen earth because they cannot stand erect in the Arctic wind, its shack-hamlets submerged in snow, its Northern Lights, and all the other things you do not meet with anywhere else. Sometimes they painted a beautiful or an original picture. Most of the time they were blazing the way for others: opening up the Canadian scene – for I am sure Jackson did not expect his school to end with the 'Seven'.

The members of this group are dispersed, have 'gone west', have disappeared or died. Only Jackson is left. He had much to do with starting it all: now he stands alone in Toronto before his easel, in the Studio-building in the Ravine, painting doggedly, the 'grand old man' of Canadian painting.

Canada will always be so infinitely bigger physically than the small nation that lives in it, even if its population is doubled, that this monstrous, empty, habitat must continue to dominate it psychologically, and so culturally, as I started by saying. The Northland, as they call it, the 'forty miles of white water', the 'beaver ponds', the virgin beauty of Mississauga, these are what cause us to give Thomson a hearing, for his crude song. It is not generally realised how at a relatively short distance north of the cities strung out across Canada in a wavering line the 'bush', the wilderness, begins, with its multitudes of lakes and streams. But Jackson went much farther afield even than Thomson: to Great Bear Lake and to the Polar Sea, and brought back grisly records of what he had seen.

With Alec Jackson I will bring this article to a close, for he interests me the most. He is himself like a bit of nature – and I have explained how it is the nature we see in them, however imperfectly, that gives them their real significance – and the rock is always more important than the man. And with Jackson let me associate Gagnon, as the French and English are conjoined in their native Quebec.

French Canada had in Clarence Gagnon, who died in 1942, a sort of national painter. These two artists are very different, though superficially their canvases have a kind of family look. Both come from the province of Quebec; in the pictures of both there is a lot of snow. There the similarity ends. Whereas Gagnon painted very attractively (mostly in his studio in Paris) an exotic world of brightly-clad peasant-puppets, in their snowbound hamlet, Jackson paints the same little Quebec hamlet for preference deserted, battened down, all but submerged in the white pest of the Canadian winter. Gagnon's is an innocuous snow, almost as if it were a stylistic device of nature (a very good-natured nature!) But Jackson's is like a white lava to smother and blot out. It is not even white! Often it is a depressing spectral grey, or acidly greenish: not at all like the sparkling blue-and-white of the icing merchants (among whom it would be unfair to count Gagnon).

The village is not where Jackson is most at home. He has painted some excellent villages: but where there are few signs of man is where he really likes to be. Where there is just Jackson and Nature. 'Nature' for Jackson does not mean what it did for Turner, a colossal and sumptuous pipe-dream akin to the Kubla Khan of Coleridge, nor what it was to Van Gogh, a barbaric tapestry, at the heart of which was man and his suffering – his human rhythms branching out, the tormented nervous system of nature responding to man's emotions. In Jackson's case it is nature-the-enemy as known to the explorer.

Yes, it is an affair of Jackson-against-nature, and vice-versa. Jackson being what is called a 'fighter' likes this situation. His painting expeditions are as it were *campaigning seasons*, rather than the breathless rendezvous of a 'nature-lover' with the object of his cult. It is impossible to associate the notion of pleasure with these grim excursions, or at least nothing sensuous. If anything there is too little that is sensuous; he handles nature roughly. Few have tried to paint the snow. These snowscapes of his fill one with the fascinating ennui of a chapter of the log of a polar-explorer: one of those grand monotonous books where one wonders how many more hundreds of pages must be traversed or trudged through (on seal-meat and pemmican) before one reaches that extraordinary over-rated abstraction the Pole.

There is gaiety sometimes in Jackson, but it is rationed. His vision is as austere as his subject-matter, which is precisely the hard puritanic land in which he always has lived: with no frills, with all its dismal solitary grandeur and bleak beauty, its bad side deliberately selected rather than its chilly relentings. This is a matter of temperament: Jackson is no man to go gathering nuts in May. He has no wish to be seduced every Spring when the sap rises – neither he nor nature are often shown in these compromising moods. There is something of Ahab in him; the long white contours of the Laurentian Mountains in midwinter are his elusive leviathan.

Select Bibliography

Atanassova, Katerina
F.H. Varley: Portraits into the Light, Toronto: Dundurn Press, 2006.

Buchanan, Donald W.
'The Story of Canadian art', *Canadian Geographical Journal*, vol. 17, no. 6, 1938.

Buchanan, Donald W.
Moderne Canadese schilderkunst, exh. cat., Groninger Museum, 12 December 1958 – 12 January 1959, Groningen, 1958.

Christensen, Lisa
A Hiker's Guide to the Rocky Mountain Art of Lawren Harris, Calgary: Fifth House Publishing, 2000.

Davies, Blodwen
Tom Thomson: The Story of a Man Who Looked for Beauty and for Truth in the Wilderness, Vancouver: Mitchell Press, 1967.

Grigor, Angela Nairne
Arthur Lismer, Visionary Art Educator, Montreal: McGill-Queen's University Press, 2002.

Harris, Bess and R. G. P. Colgrove eds.
Lawren Harris, Toronto: MacMillan, 1969.

Harris, Lawren
'The Story of the Group of Seven', in *Group of Seven*, exh. cat., Vancouver Art Gallery, 1954.

Hill, Charles C., and Dennis Reid, eds.
Tom Thomson, exh. cat., Vancouver/Toronto: Douglas & McIntyre with the Art Gallery of Ontario and National Gallery of Canada, 2002.

Hill, Charles C.
Terre sauvage: Canadian Landscape Painting and the Group of Seven, exh. cat., National Gallery of Canada, Ottawa, 1999. *The Group of Seven: Art for a Nation*, exh. cat., National Gallery of Canada, Ottawa, 1995.

Housser, F. B.
A Canadian Art Movement: The Story of the Group of Seven, Toronto: Macmillan, 1926.

Jackson, A.Y.
A Painter's Country: The Autobiography of A.Y. Jackson, Toronto: Clarke, Irwin & Co. Ltd, 1958, memorial edition 1976.

King, Ross
Defiant Spirits: The Modernist Revolution of the Group of Seven, exh. cat., Vancouver/Toronto: Douglas & McIntyre with the McMichael Canadian Art Collection, 2010.

Larisey, Peter
Light for a Cold Land: Lawren Harris's Work and Life – An Interpretation, Toronto: Dundurn Press, 1993.

MacGregor, Roy
Northern Light, Toronto: Vintage Books Canada, 2010.

Mastin, Catharine M., ed.
The Group of Seven in Western Canada, Toronto: Key Porter; Calgary: Glenbow Museum, 2002.

Mellen, Peter
The Group of Seven, Toronto: McClelland & Stewart, 1970.

Nasgaard, Roald
The Mystic North: Symbolist Landscape Painting in Northern Europe and North America 1890–1940, Toronto: University of Toronto Press, 1984.

O'Brian, John and Peter White
Beyond Wilderness: The Group of Seven, Canadian Identity, and Contemporary Art, Montreal/Kingston: McGill-Queen's University Press, 2007.

Silcox, David P.
The Group of Seven and Tom Thomson, Toronto: Firefly Books, 2003.

Tippett, Maria
Stormy Weather, F.H. Varley, A Biography, Toronto: McClelland & Stewart, 1998.

Tooby, Michael (ed.)
The True North: Canadian Landscape Painting 1896–1939, exh. cat., Lund Humphries, London, in association with Barbican Art Gallery, 1991.

Town, Harold and David P. Silcox
Tom Thomson: The Silence and the Storm, 4th rev. edn, Toronto: Firefly Books, 2001.

Wyndham Lewis, Percy
'Canadian nature and its painters', *The Listener*, vol. XXXVI, no. 920, 29th August 1946.

Image Credits

Index